LITTLE KNOWN TALES IN CALIFORNIA HISTORY

By Alton Pryor

D0028972

Stagecoach Publishing
Roseville, California

Little Known Tales in California History

ISBN: 0-9660053-1-7
First Edition

First Printing, 1997
Second Printing, 1998
Third Printing, 1998

Stagecoach Publishing

5360 Campcreek Loop
Roseville, Ca. 95747
Phone (916) 771-8166

Little Known

Tales

in

California History

*Truth is the
only merit that
gives dignity
and worth to
history.*
      Lord Acton

To my wife, Edie,
for her encouragement
and to my son, Scott,
who helped steer the
way to completion.

History is the living past of the dead, not the dead past of the living.

Table of Contents

Acknowledgement

I wish to express especial thanks to
Erin Fulkerson
for her beautiful and descriptive art
work. Erin is a freelance artist
living in Roseville, California.

Preface

These brief tales are instant history lessons for those who are newcomers to the golden state as well as those who have lived here for years but never caught up with California history.

The author has attempted to include a wide selection of factual articles that illustrate the diverse people and the events which settled California.

As the reader will soon note, not all of those early-day pioneers were heroic. There were scoundrels mixed in among the righteous.

This history is intended as a series of "five-minute" history lessons that will give the reader a better grasp of some aspects of California's development, and we hope, a lot of enjoyable reading.

Alton Pryor

Chapter 1

'Lucky' Baldwin

'He Knew How to Make a Buck'

Lucky Baldwin came south from San Francisco with millions in his deep pockets. His early fortune, which he made after arriving in California, came from a number of sources, including poker, horse racing and horse trading, mining shares, real estate, and other less legitimate enterprises.

> *"His name is known throughout the sporting world, but I never knew but one good thing him; he never threw a race."*
> Edward Morphy
> Editor, The California Turf

"To be a success," Elias Jackson "Lucky" Baldwin philosophized, "you've got to keep your eye on two ends---when to go in and when to go out---and don't waste any time doing either."

He despised the "Lucky" sobriquet that had been pinned on him. He insisted that everything he had achieved was the fruit of his own labor. There was no such thing as "luck" to Lucky.

Baldwin landed in San Francisco in 1853 with seven thousand dollars in his pocket. Almost immediately, he could see there was a lack of living facilities in the city, either for men, or for their horses.

After spending a few days in the badly managed Pacific Temperance Hotel, Baldwin was sure he could run the place better. The proprietor said he would sell the hotel for six thousand dollars. Baldwin offered him five thousand.

> *"With twenty million dollars worth of property, "Lucky" Baldwin was always broke."*
> W.A. Chess
> Monrovia bank cashier

The proprietor asked, "Supposing I had asked five thousand?"

Baldwin glibly answered, "Then I would have offered you four."

After coming to an agreement three days later, Baldwin wrote out a check for five thousand dollars. As he did so, however, he asked a favor. "Could I date the check and the bill of sale three days earlier so I can show the folks back home what a speedy operator I really am"? The proprietor agreed.

But no sooner was the signing completed, when Baldwin said, "And now, there is a little matter of three days' board and lodging."

"Oh, yes," said the hotel man, "you do owe me for three days board and room."

"On the contrary," countered Baldwin. "You owe me. According to this check and agreement, I have owned the hotel for three days."

17

A month after he had bought the hotel, Baldwin sold it, doubling his money for a profit of five thousand dollars.

The horse-loving Lucky then opened two riding stables. He eventually decided to sell one of them. He found a prospective buyer and gave him a thirty-day option, after which time the buyer, if satisfied, could buy the stable for ten thousand dollars.

> *"I believe I am the only man who ever collected a bill from "Lucky" Baldwin without a court judgement."*
> Will E. Keller
> Grain Broker

Baldwin then rushed to deflect all of the business from the stable he retained, to that of the hopeful buyer. When business exceeded the buyer's most optimistic hopes, he gladly paid Lucky the ten thousand dollar asking price.

But the gullible buyer had no sooner received the bill of sale than business at his newly bought stable fell off. As soon as the deal had closed, Lucky had diverted the business back to his own stable.

During his travels to southern California, Lucky fell in love with the Santa Anita Rancho, just east of Pasadena. This oak studded valley measured about twelve square miles and had a view of the ocean.

He wanted that property. Someone told him it could be purchased for a small price. The property belonged to H. Newmark & Company, and consisted of more than eight thousand acres. Newmark had paid $85,000 for the rancho.

On Lucky's first visit to Newmark's office, he offered the owner of the Santa Anita Rancho $150,000. Newmark informed him the price was $175,000, and Baldwin left in a huff, declaring he would be at the Bella Union should the price be lowered. Newmark did not show up.

Swallowing his pride, Baldwin returned to Newmark's office. "The price is now $200,000," the land owner said, and a week from today, it will cost you $225,000."

> "Baldwin was a kind man, and a great man, in spite of anything. He'd have made me rich if I'd had sense enough to let him."
> J.I. Fisher
> A Baldwin employee for 37 years.

Reuben Lloyd, a San Francisco attorney who had accompanied Baldwin to Newmark's office, knew how much Lucky wanted that ranch, and knew also that Baldwin could afford it. He urged Lucky to reconsider.

"Lucky, go back and buy that ranch," Lloyd told him, "or they'll raise the price on you!"

Four days later, Baldwin returned to purchase the property, carrying a tin box. "The price is now $225,000," Newmark informed Baldwin.

"Sir," sputtered Baldwin, "it isn't next week yet." Newmark admitted he had made a mistake and agreed to take $175,000. Baldwin withdrew $12,500 from the metal box, offering it as a down payment.

According to an account by Newmark himself, in his book, "Sixty Years in Southern California," the tin

19

box may have contained several million dollars, as he had glimpsed five million in gold bank notes while the box lay open on his desk.

In a deal soon after the Santa Anita Rancho purchase, Lucky Baldwin loaned $210,000 to Temple and Workman, owners of a Los Angeles bank that was in financial trouble.

Baldwin demanded the men give him, as collateral, a blanket-mortgage on their combined real estate. This included Workman's Puento Rancho, and Temple's La Merced Rancho.

In addition, Baldwin wanted a mortgage on the property of Juan Matias Sanchez, a friend of Workman and Temple whose 2,200-acre holdings was the finest land around the Old Mission.

> *"Baldwin sacrificed a profit of $18,000,000 for one of $5,000,000 to prevent a panic in the days of the big bonanza."*
> H.H. Bancroft
> Author, "Chronicles of the Builders"

Lucky had known even better than the bank owners themselves how shaky their financial firm was. He also knew they would never be able to pay off the mortgages he now held on the three properties.

Baldwin foreclosed on the three properties, making him the owner of a feudal estate unmatched in California, totaling some 60,000 acres in all.

Temple and Sanchez both died ruined men, having lost their land to Baldwin. Workman soon committed suicide.

Lucky Baldwin also took on the giant railroads. One special issue was his confrontation with Santa Fe Railroad. Baldwin had given three railroad rights of way across his ranch, with the written stipulation that all trains were to stop on his signal. He especially liked the Santa Fe Super Chief.

Baldwin and his entourage, in the summer of 1900, returned from a trip in the mountains. He walked up to the clerk in an isolated way station, and asked for express tickets to Santa Anita.

The agent steadfastly informed him, "The express does not stop either at this station or at Santa Anita."

Baldwin struck the counter with his cane and demanded a telegraph blank. He addressed a message to his ranch foreman: "Put two hundred men to work at once tearing up Santa Fe's tracks through my ranch---E.J. Baldwin."

The station agent hastily backed off as he read Lucky's message, and quickly made out the tickets--- "Destination: Santa Anita".

> *"He loved to be fussed over and made much of. He was like a child in that, and he couldn't do too much for those who showed him pleasant attentions."*
> Mrs. Rosebudd Doble Mullender
> Baldwin's granddaughter

But Lucky Baldwin's real interests, other than money, were women and horses. To him, both were unusually fast.

21

He built Santa Anita Racetrack on a portion of his ranch. He won races on all of America's tracks and women found him and his money irresistible. At least one woman with whom he tired is said to have taken pistol shots at him. None of these attempts caused injury.

Baldwin's income was estimated at $200,000 a month.. When he died, his estate was worth more than twenty million dollars. Even so, Baldwin never paid a debt without a court judgement, and he never paid a judgement if there was some way around it.

> *"Lucky" Baldwin's reputation must survive for generations to come as that of one of the greatest pioneers of the west, the greatest builders of California, the most spectacular of libertines, and the most contradictory of characters in our annals."*
> Arthur M. Ellis
> Historical Society of Southern California

One artist, whom Baldwin hired by verbal contract to paint pictures of his valuable horses, had to sue for the fee. He eventually compromised by accepting one tenth of the agreed upon thirty thousand dollars.

Lucky wasn't without his largesse, however. When the adjoining town of Monrovia needed twice the number of children it had in order to get state aid for a public school, Baldwin accommodated.

He moved fifteen of his Mexican families into the district, and had the children counted as residents, even though the parents returned each day to Santa Anita.

While Baldwin spurned his "Lucky" nickname, luck did play a role in his fortunes. It was one streak of luck that earned him a great deal of money. He had forgotten to sell a sheaf of mining stock he thought was overpriced.

A year later, Lucky found the sheaf of stock still in his safe deposit box. The value had increased by more than one hundred thousand dollars.

Lucky Baldwin died in 1909 at the age of eighty-one.

Chapter 2

The Lost Spanish Galleon

'It still lies on the bottom of the   Salton Sea'

A tale that has grown with each telling is that of the Lost Spanish Galleon. It is a story told by Cahuilla Indians.

The Salton Sea was once five to six times its present size. The sea was said to have stretched from Indio all the way to the border of Mexico.

Indians sailed the sea with their tule rafts to snare waterfowl. These rafts were the only watercraft used on the sea. It was a sea without ships.

Cahuillas standing on the shore one day spotted what seemed a mirage, off to the south. The vision shimmered cloud-like in the distance. As the object gradually moved closer, the Cahuillas saw it was not a mirage at all, but a craft that floated across the sea, much like their own rafts, but much larger with white wings to catch the winds.

Hidden behind rocks, the Cahuillas watched the strange craft as it floated closer to their village. As the vessel came to a stop, the Indians could discern men aboard, walking briskly about. They watched an object being thrown into the water, making a huge splash. The great white wings were then folded, letting the ship stand still.

The Cahuillas could hear the voices of the men aboard. Sumai, chief of the Cahuillas, cautioned his people to remain hidden because the voices were those of Spaniards, which he had heard during a trip to the south as a young man.

The Indians went back to their village and held council throughout the night. The older men, who had heard of Spanish greed, wanted to take the women and children and flee into the mountains. But the younger men, proud of their heritage as warriors, prevailed.

Instead of running, they wanted to attack the Spaniards as they came ashore, although they knew these strange visitors would probably offer gifts and profess peace.

In the morning, some of the older tribal men crept to the point where the Spaniards were moored. They watched in silence while a single Indian and ten of the other men lowered a small boat, armed with muskets, and poled toward the shore.

The Indian interpreter aboard hailed the Cahuillas on shore. He was of the Yuma tribe, he told them. He pointed to one of the bearded men in the boat, explaining that he was Captain Moreno, the Son of the Sun, and was coming to greet the Cahuillas.

A wary Indian on shore asked, "Why, if he is the 'Son of the Sun', is he not able to speak for himself rather than through an interpreter?"

The Yuma interpreter dismissed the question, asking if the Cahuillas had any gold that they wished to give to the Son of the Sun. They replied they had much gold, when, in fact, they had very little. The gold was in the village, they lied. It was only a short distance away, beyond the spur of the mountain where the chief of the Cahuillas was now waiting.

After discussing the Yuma Indian's translation of what had been said, the Spaniards gave each of the Indians a handful of trinkets and asked them to bring their chief to the ship where they could entertain him and give him valuable gifts.

The Cahuillas answered that their chief was sick. In order to see him, the Spaniards would have to go to the village, but it would be best to do so the following day. Most of the tribe, they fibbed, was in the mountains hunting deer and would be greatly downcast at not seeing the Son of the Sun.

After discussing the Cahuillas suggestion, the Spaniards shouted to the men still on the ship. Soon after, another boat was dispatched for shore, carrying nine more men, all of them armed.

The Yuma translated. "The Son of the Sun was sorry, but he would be unable to wait until the next day. He wished to be taken to the chief immediately and by the shortest way.

In single file, the Cahuillas leading, they entered a narrow defile strewn with large boulders that served as a natural gateway to the village. Young warriors from the village were hidden behind boulders on both sides of the trail, ready to attack the alien seamen.

When the Spaniards were well within the defile, more than fifty Indians fell upon them, dividing the party into two. The Spanish seamen had no chance to discharge their weapons and little time to use them as clubs. In a matter of minutes, they were all beaten to death with rocks.

The Yuma interpreter, too, was killed in the melee.

The Cahuillas had no way of knowing how many men remained aboard the Spanish galleon, so they decided to attack the ship in the dark of the night. The number aboard was thought to be small, fewer perhaps, than the number that had been killed.

As darkness fell, the Cahuillas assembled their rafts, loaded them with warriors, and cautiously poled toward the ship.

They searched for the rope they had seen dangling from the bow and by which the Spaniards had lowered themselves. Three Cahuillas, carrying clubs fastened to their belts, scampered up the rope and onto the deck. Others swarmed after them, and more followed still when they heard the clash of muskets above the sound of the wind.

The Cahuillas and the seamen fought through the night. At dawn, many Cahuillas were dead or injured. There were no Spaniards alive. All had been killed and tossed into the sea.

The victors had already began the looting of the vessel. Cahuilla warriors were running about in a frenzy with their arms full of silk shawls and ivory fans. Others struggled with iron chests that were impossible to unlock and too heavy to lift.

Now the Cahuillas were faced with a different danger. The wind had increased during the night and a violent Santana began buffeting the ship. No one aboard knew how to manage the craft.

Some of the rafts below loosened from their moorings, floating out of reach of the warriors. Those who could reach the rafts did so, while the rest simply jumped into the sea, carrying their loot with them. The ship lurched away in the wind, drifting into the west.

As the Cahuillas watched the craft drifting across the water, they hoped the wind would carry it to the far shore where it would land on the beach. This would allow the Indians to explore its contents further, and to open those giant iron chests they had not been able to unlock.

After drifting no further than a league, the ship, without warning, turned over, and slowly sank.

When the Santana wind abated, the Cahuillas searched for the ship, but it had sunken too deep even for their best divers. The galleon remained there throughout the generation of the tribe and throughout the next generation as well.

Then, when the banks of the Colorado River began to shift, and the Salton Sea gradually began to dry up, hopes of finding the ship sprung anew in the Cahuillas. When the dry land reached the point where the ship should lay, it was no longer visible, but buried under tons of silt.

The Cahuillas continued digging for the ship for years without success. Finally, they ended their search, admitting failure.

In modern times, adventurous Americans have taken up the search, extending the area of operations to include most of the Coachella Valley.

It is believed the Spanish galleon was a ship bound out from the Philippines for the port of Acapulco.

While the Cahuillas did not find a fortune on the Spanish galleon, they did win a financial suit with the U.S. government. After World War II, a series of legal claims were lodged against the federal government by Indians throughout the nation.

The Supreme Court awarded the 71 surviving members of the Cahuilla tribe some land in the Valley. The Indians remained unsatisfied with the settlement, and Congress, in 1959, passed an additional law giving the Cahuillas in excess of 30,000 acres.

The Indians thus achieved a commanding position in real estate ownership in the popular and wealthy Palm Springs vacation spa.

Chapter 3

Pegleg Smith's Lost Gold Mine

'He found gold, and then could never find his way back'

Thomas L. "Pegleg" Smith was not a quitter. For years he searched for the mountain of gold he had discovered while lost in a sandstorm. Adventurous prospectors still seek the illusive location.

Smith was the son of Irish immigrants, born in Kentucky October 10, 1801. At 16, he ran away from home, joining the crew of a Mississippi riverboat. Never one to idle, he fled a smallpox epidemic in New Orleans and headed north on the Cherokee Trail.

He had a run-in with pirates, one of whom he killed, and then lived with the Chickasaw Indians for a full year. He later worked as a riverboat hand as well as a saloon keeper in St. Louis.

At the age of 22, Smith joined a caravan at Santa Fe, and then went to Utah where he became a trapper. He wasted little time in gaining a stronger reputation as a "trafficker" in horses and as a fighter.

Pegleg got his nickname while officiating at the burial of a partner who was killed by Indians in a horse stealing foray. During that incident, Smith was shot in the leg by an arrow, breaking the large bone.

According to legend he cut the muscles in his own leg in aiding an amateur frontier surgeon with the amputation.

Smith felt more comfortable with the Indians than with his white brethren. After his serious leg wound, he returned to the tribe to rest from his frontier surgery. While with the Indians, he whittled a wooden pegleg from an oak sapling. This piece of wood served him well, both as a leg and as a weapon in many later encounters.

Pegleg could never relocate the three buttes
he had used as a landmark.

In 1829, the adventurous Pegleg journeyed down the Colorado River, trapping along the way as he continued toward the legendary gold country of the desert. It is at this point that the tale of Pegleg's gold begins.

Caught in a blinding sand storm, Pegleg lost his way. He was miserably lost and climbed the highest hump he could find to survey his surroundings. He needed to get his bearings and, hopefully, spot where water might be located.

Pegleg remembered seeing three buttes sticking up on the horizon. But it was the color of the hill on which he stood that really sparked his interest. The base was a chalky yellow color while the summit was black. The hill was literally covered with odd, round-shaped stones, the size of walnuts.

These stones were black and heavy. He put a few of the rocks in his pocket, then went to sleep so he could get an early start the next morning.

When Pegleg had the stones assayed at Temecula, he learned the black obsidian-like rocks were pure gold. He had thought they were copper, which he had seen in Arizona.

Brash in his youth, instead of immediately returning to the site, Pegleg continued to trap, drink, fight and carouse. But word of this first great California gold strike rang out from Temecula and around the world.

Pegleg eventually came to his senses, and organized an expedition, using Warner Springs as a starting point. He had few facts to rely on in finding his lost gold mine. The only real thing he knew was his starting point the day he walked through the sand storm and found the oddly shaped stones.

He only knew there were high mountains to the northwest, and there were three distinctive buttes.

Pegleg was later seen searching at the Mud Pots below Salton Sea, in the hills south of the Santa Rosa Mountains, around Carrizo Canyon, and at Warner's

Ranch, never again finding that elusive spot where he had gathered the golden stones.

With disappointment, he discontinued his search, travelling north where his Indian friends made him a Blackfoot Chief, and supplied him with a number of squaws.

Pegleg's wild career then becomes confusing. It's known he participated in horse stealing raids on the early Spanish ranchos. He continued a thriving, although outlaw business, bartering both horses and liquor among the Indians and the early travelers.

Later, in the 1850s, Pegleg was seen in Hangtown (now Placerville), with his half-breed son, indulging in his favorite sports of gambling, fighting, and drinking.

Although Pegleg's reputation was bad, his courage was never questioned. Interestingly, after California seceded from Mexico, he never again led an attack against the ranchos.

The legend of the three golden buttes has not only survived through the years, but has grown in its retelling. Prospectors built a monument of loose rocks in Borrego Valley to Pegleg's memory. Some, who continued searching for the path to the lost mine, lost their lives to the cruel and inhumane desert.

Others carefully reenacted the very details and conditions under which Pegleg traveled when he found the odd, walnut-like stones. All these efforts proved fruitless, but countless other optimistic prospectors continued the quest for the lost Pegleg gold.

Some gold seekers tried travelling during the same blinding sandstorms, with burros, and other props, just as Pegleg had traveled. They were never able to locate those three elusive buttes.

There are few detractors to the story. Most prospectors do indeed believe the truth of Pegleg's lost gold mine.

Stories abound about the black nuggets in the desert. One tale concerns a soldier discharged from Fort Yuma, who reportedly discovered Pegleg's black, walnut-sized rocks.

The soldier later returned with two companions to look for more gold. The skeletons of the three were found in the San Ysidro foothills some thirty miles west of the Salton Sea.

A Yaqui Indian, employed at Warner's Ranch, would disappear for several days before any local celebration. When he returned, he had plenty of gold to spend on a good time, never bothering to get good value for his lava covered nuggets. He knew where to find more.

Attempts to follow the Indian to his Golden Horde were futile. The cagey Indian would enter the Pegleg region of desert and was never gone more than three days.

Even Governor Downey, owner of Warner's Ranch, went to the ranch to interview the Yaqui. Before the governor arrived, however, the Indian was killed while on a spree in Anaheim. Four thousand dollars in coarse gold was found in his bunk.

The Yaqui's squaw, Carmelita, was closely questioned by the governor. She explained that her buck got his last water at the spring of the White Ledge before entering the desert. He always left the water hole at daybreak, travelling toward the sun until about three o'clock in the afternoon, when he would come to "mucho, mucho gold", she said.

Many believe the White Ledge Carmelita referred to was the "sweet water" Pegleg Smith had referred to, and which is now called Borrego Springs.

Later, Carmelita would likewise disappear into the desert, much as her husband had, never telling anyone where she was going. The squaw always had sufficient gold to satisfy her needs.

Still another Indian woman is said to have staggered into the Salton Station in an exhausted condition. Her tongue swollen from thirst, the woman could barely babble out that her buck had perished in the trip across the desert.

She said her husband, after wandering off the trail, became confused. They, too, as had Pegleg Smith, climbed one of "tres poco picachos", (three small peaks), to regain their bearing.

The squaw said once they were atop the hill, they found nuggets, and the woman had several pounds of them when she reached Salton Station. She was the third person to describe the three buttes that remain a mystery in the Pegleg gold.

Dozens of stories have continued pouring in from people claiming to have found the Pegleg gold. None, thus far, have been able to find their way to the site again. Ralph L. Caine, in his book, "Lost Desert Gold", lists a host of stories surrounding the Pegleg gold. The search goes on.

Chapter 4

Joaquin Murrieta

'Was he only a myth in western folk lore?'

In 1848, there were two rival gold camps, one at Angel's Camp and the other at San Andreas. The San Andreas mine was founded by Mexican prospectors, and it turned out to be a rich mine.

American miners considered the Mexicans an inferior breed and not worthy of such a rich claim. Twenty-one miners from the Angel's Camp mine poured into the camp of San Andreas, driving the Mexican miners out.

Thereby hangs the tale of Joaquin Murrieta, considered one of California's most notorious bandits.

The fiery tempered Americans descended on Joaquin's camp, and hung Murrieta's brother for a crime he had not committed. They also horsewhipped Joaquin and raped the outlaw's girlfriend, Mariana.

This incident so outraged Joaquin, he took to the outlaw trail. He became one of the west's most talked about outlaws. Joaquin became a legend equal to another notorious bandit at that time, Tiburcio Vasquez.

There is a difference between the two banditos, however. There are police records to authenticate the many crimes of Vasquez, but no such records exist on Joaquin Murrieta.

Joaquin formed a band of cutthroats to prey on American settlements after the death of his brother. Joaquin and his gang traced down and eventually brought all 21 Americans involved in murdering his brother to justice. Joaquin himself dispatched 19 of them.

Some historians consider Joaquin a myth, created in the fertile brain of newspaper reporter John Rollin Ridge, who, in 1854, wrote what was designated as "The Life and Adventures of Joaquin Murieta". Ridge was a part-time miner, auditor, recorder, deputy county clerk, poet, and newspaper writer.

Whichever story holds true, Joaquin was considered the most notorious bandit in the Mother Lode Country. To his Mexican brethren, he became something of a Robin Hood of the West.

Joaquin's first outlaw escapade, in which he dispatched the killers of his brother, aroused the Calaveras community. They held mass meetings, passing resolutions in which all Mexicans were ordered to leave the county. At the same time, civilian posses scoured the region for outlaws.

At one point, three Mexicans, supposedly part of Joaquin's band, were unceremoniously hanged. Bands of Americans drove the Mexican population from San Andreas and the upper Calaveras River.

A Stockton newspaper account reported, "If an American meets a Mexican, he takes his horse, his arms, and bids him to leave."

As the pressure against all Mexicans increased, Joaquin and his band decided to head north. They robbed as they went. At one point, they attacked a Chinese camp, massacring six people and making off with $6,000.

Three of the Murrieta band were captured near Fiddletown and forced to depart on a single horse, two riding and the other running behind while hanging onto the horse's tail.

Atrocities laid at the hands of Joaquin and his gang continued, angering government officials as well as residents.

Some say Joaquin Murrieta's mustache continued to grow after twenty state rangers brought his severed head back in a pickle jar full of brandy. (California State Library)

Finally, Governor John Bigler authorized Captain Harry Love, a former Mexican War express rider, and now a California peace officer, to take 20 rangers and bring Joaquin to justice.

The rangers caught up with Joaquin and his band near the town of Coalinga. In the ensuing battle, Joaquin was killed.

To prove the deed was done, Love and his rangers carried back the head of Joaquin, along with the deformed hand of "Three-Fingered Jack", a member of the Murrieta gang.

Both the head and the hand were preserved in a keg of brandy (although other accounts say it was a pickle jar). The head was exhibited in a San Francisco museum later destroyed in the Great Earthquake and Fire of 1906.

Some accounts maintain that Joaquin's fierce mustache continued to lengthen as the head floated in the jar over the years.

Other skeptics insisted the head in the pickle jar was not that of Joaquin at all. These doubters pointed to the fact that Joaquin was comparatively light complexioned, showing a high degree of Spanish blood.

The head in the brandy appeared to be of an older man with a swarthy complexion. History never truly determined that it was indeed the head of the bandit. Some who claimed to have known Joaquin back in Calaveras County, said the head was not that of Joaquin at all.

Adding to the claims of the doubters, it was duly noted the pickled head was never placed on exhibit in Calaveras County where he would have been more readily recognized.

Fiction writers have muddied the Joaquin Murrieta waters even more over the years, adding their own figments of imagination to "el bandido magnifico", the Bandit of the El Dorado.

As historian Angus MacLean said in his book, "Legends of the California Banditos," it is just as well that Joaquin's true escapades remain unknown. "It is doubtful if the real-life Murrieta could ever have been as intriguing as the legendary one."

Contributing to the doubts that Murrieta ever existed are the variations in spelling of his name by various historians, alternating between Murrieta and Murrietta with an extra "t", as well Murieta, with a single "r", as it was in Ridge's 1854 book.

The name of his girlfriend, too, has been variously listed as Rosita, Rosalisa, Carmela, Carmen, Clarinda, Clarita, and Mariana.

Back in 1853, there were reports from Americanos in El Pueblo de San Luis Obispo that Joaquin and his band rode into the little town, forcibly taking over the mission gardens and campground.

The townspeople were so convinced it was Murrieta, they hid in the basement of a store, staying off the streets for two or three days until the outlaw band moved on. Joaquin Murrieta's capture and death is supposed to have happened July 25, 1853.

Detractors of Ridge's book point out there is little in contemporary accounts to substantiate the tale of Joaquin Murrieta. It is noted, as well, that few newspaper reporters at the time had much chance to obtain first-hand information for their papers.

The saga of Joaquin Murrieta seems more placed in word-of-mouth accounts than in solid, written records. Some versions passed down in the folklore say that Murrieta, recognizing the futileness of his cause, gathered up his loot and headed for Mexico. Some old-timers even claimed to have seen him in later years.

There are other tales that maintain Joaquin had been put to a grisly torture death by some traitors in his outlaw band some weeks before Harry Love's rangers claimed to have find and killed him.

This version has been attributed to Mariana Murrieta, the "widow" of Joaquin. Often called Mariana La Loca by her fellow townsmen, she was said to willingly tell different versions of Joaquin's death in exchange for money.

Further, she often stated, it was she that had found the mutilated body of Joaquin, the head still intact, which she buried near a tree in Cantua Canyon.

Joaquin's outlaw career, if true, covered less than three years and he was little known outside his own small circle of confederates. Whatever the truth, Joaquin Murrieta has survived, becoming a folk hero in both California and Mexican lore.

Chapter 5

Lord George Gordon

'The impeccable promoter'

Lord George Gordon was indeed a dapper promoter. He could con the feathers from a rooster. He dressed with impeccable taste, spoke with an English accent, and considered himself something of a Beau Brummell of the Western world.

Some said he was not a lord at all, and even questioned his British birth and English accent. Others were even more unkind, suggesting he was born in New York's Bowery.

George's first American adventure was to charter a ship to bring gold seekers from the east coast around the horn to San Francisco.

He signed up two hundred gold-hungry recruits for the trip, telling them they would sail in luxury from New York to California for the easy sum of one hundred and sixty dollars.

His only profit, he assured them, would not be made by the passenger fares, but by taking twenty percent of the gold that each of the voyagers took from the California hills.

Gordon's luxury sailing vessel turned out to be a wreck of a ship with no sleeping accommodations and little food. While the passengers were crowded into quarters without bunks, Lord George was travelling

42

overland with more than thirty thousand dollars the gold seekers had paid him for fare. There are no records indicating the vessel ever arrived at San Francisco.

This didn't end Lord George's escapades. Once in San Francisco, he set about planning more elaborate schemes.

Lord George proposed to banker Harry Meiggs that he and his friends give Gordon enough money to terrace Telegraph Hill and turn it into another Italian Riviera. There would be trees, shaded walks, monuments, and fountains.

Mr. Meiggs was not so easily taken in as the gold seekers. He informed Gordon, in no uncertain terms, that he, personally, didn't give a continental damn about beautifying the city. He only wanted to make money.

Lord George was not to be deterred. He suggested exactly how Mr. Meiggs could make money. They could build a great wharf where the waters flowing through the Golden Gate joined the waters of San Francisco Bay. The wharf, incidentally, would be called Meigg's Wharf.

This, Mr. Meiggs thought, did have a happy ring to it. And the fact that Meigg's Wharf would be the first name to greet incoming travelers interested the banker even more.

Lord George Gordon built Meigg's Wharf with a tidy profit for himself. History later records that Meiggs, himself, however, turned out to be a thief who absconded with funds belonging to several San Francisco widows and orphans.

Lord George had a miserable home life, having gotten entangled in a marriage to an alcoholic barmaid while still a young man in England. To escape this situation, he plunged into other ventures.

He started importing and refining sugar. Gordon built the first sugar refinery in northern California, making a considerable fortune. This sugar refinery became the nucleus of the vast Spreckels empire, who purchased Gordon's interests.

George was not done with his promotional talents, however. He envisioned developing some of the large acreage standing idle on the Peninsula, where William D.S. Howard and others had acquired great land grants from Mexico.

Lord George just knew the Peninsula could be transformed into the fashion center of the west. He purchased a tract of land there and built a fine home.

This home later became the residence of Senator and Mrs. Leland Stanford. The great acres, which Gordon had purchased, became the site of Stanford University.

Gordon never gave up on his idea of beautifying Telegraph Hill. Taking an architect with him, he walked across Market Street to the sand dunes at the edge of the bay. It was a dismal, windswept waste of sand.

"Isn't it beautiful?" George beamed to the aghast architect. "There lies the beauty spot of the Western world---a gentleman's paradise! And we're going to build it."

When the architect responded that San Francisco needed a place for mud-grimed miners rather than a gentleman's paradise, George had a ready response.

"Mud-grimed miners become rich men. And rich men demand a paradise."

George described his plan. He would build a park at the base of Rincon Hill. There would be an oval garden with a high grille fence, much like London's residential parks. An artistic iron gate would stand at each corner of the park, and the park would be surrounded by fashionable, London-style houses.

Gordon's dream did become reality. Clipper ships came around the horn bearing English furniture and carpets to furnish the houses.

Men did make their fortunes in gold or in real estate property, and they came swarming with money in hand to South Park. The Hearsts, the Hall McAllisters, and others settled into the fashionable quarter.

The glory of South Park faded as warehouses and other industrial buildings were erected. Freight trains now rattle by it, and above the site stand the stone piers of the Bay Bridge.

Even though Lord George accomplished many of his fanciful dreams, his dreadful family life drove him into a funk. Some say he died of a broken heart.

Chapter 6

Rattlesnake Dick

'The pirate of the placers'

"Rattlesnake Dick" was an honest gold miner. His moniker came not from being a sneaky character, but rather from the fact he settled in an area known as Rattlesnake Bar, near Auburn.

Towns in the area carried a wide array of unusual place names, such as Shirt Tail Canyon, Humbug Bar, Milk Punch Bar, Hell's Delight, and Ladies' Canyon.

Rattlesnake Dick Barter was falsely accused twice of stealing. Otherwise he might never have become an outlaw. Even though he was exonerated from both accusations, it always galled him. He felt there was a smirch on his reputation around Rattlesnake Bar so Dick decided to change his name and move to the northern town of Shasta.

His move to Shasta, along with a name change, failed to give him the new start he wanted. A former neighbor from Rattlesnake Bar passed through Shasta and spotted Dick. He readily told the townsmen of Dick's suspect character.

"Well," Dick told himself, "if I'm going to be accused of being a thief, I might as well become one."

Dick quickly began the task of living up to his unsavory reputation. In his first outlaw episode, he pounced on a lone traveler, boasting to the victim as he left, "You have just been robbed by 'Rattlesnake Dick, the Pirate of the Placers'".

With vengeance in his heart, Dick returned to Auburn country. He would show his accusers, who had ruined his name and reputation, what a bandit he could really be. For the next six years, Rattlesnake Dick plundered the roads from Nevada City to Folsom.

Rattlesnake didn't always get away with his escapades. He was often caught and thrown in the local jail to await trial. Just as often, he proved his slipperiness by escaping his jailers.

When falsely accused of crimes he didn't commit, RattlesnakeDick decided he would live up to his outlaw reputation.

Newspaper accounts noted Rattlesnake Dick "broke out of every jail in Placer and Nevada counties". This was a little much for the staid townsmen of Auburn, where peace and quiet was more desired than was the rough-housing of other gold towns.

Rattlesnake Dick became brazen in his approach to highway robbery. He and a companion boarded a stage in Nevada City that was apparently carrying a gold shipment. While the pair calmly took their seats, the news of their boarding reached Placer County's deputy sheriff.

"Enough is enough," thought the deputy. He would stop the stage at Harmon Hill and arrest the pair.

As the deputy halted the stage, the two bandits remained calm and unimpressed.

"Would the deputy mind just showing them a warrant for their arrest?" they asked.

As the deputy reached for the warrant, Rattlesnake Dick and his partner sent a barrage of bullets through the stagecoach windows. The deputy returned fire, using a one-shot derringer.

Before the deputy could reload, the bandits departed the stage, bidding the bewildered deputy goodbye, but not without imparting a few rude remarks about his abilities. No one was injured in the incident.

As his success as a bandit grew, so did Rattlesnake's boldness. In 1859, he and another outlaw companion rode openly through the streets of Auburn, a blatant affront to this serene little town. They were accosted by a three-man posse who were

48

outraged by the effrontery of the outlaw pair. The two were ordered to halt by the posse leader.

"Who are you, and what do you want?" Dick demanded, at the same time drawing a weapon and firing.

One member of the posse was killed while the other two returned fire. A lawman's bullet hit Dick. He lurched in his saddle but managed to gallop off with his companion.

Dick's body was found the next morning by the roadside. It was carried back into town the next day by the Auburn stage.

But highway robbers just wouldn't leave the quiet town of Auburn alone. After Rattlesnake Dick's demise, highwayman Tom Bell became Auburn's nemesis.

Bell was said to be a doctor by profession, a calling at which he apparently failed. Neither did he make it as a miner or as a gambler. Failing at all else, he turned to armed robbery.

He hid out in at least three highway taverns, whose owners tipped him off on the departures of their well-heeled guests. The raids of Bell and his gang became such an outrage that lawmen in all of northern California determined to stop the lawbreakers.

When Placer County's sheriff caught up with the gang at one point, Bell slipped away, hiding out near Firebaugh's Ferry on the San Joaquin River. There, he was surprised by a posse. Taken without a fight, Bell was hung without fanfare.

This allowed Auburn to resume its former quiet and unexciting community life.

Chapter 7

The Camel Experiment

'The Army dusted off its 'Camel Corps" plan'

The cost of maintaining its army outposts across the U.S. was appalling to both Congress and the War Department.

It wasn't "wild Indians" or "renegade Mexican bandits", that ran up the costs. It was the transporting of forage and other necessary outpost items through arid and semi-arid country.

Eureka! Government officials had the ideal answer. They dusted off an old plan for a "Camel Corps". The army would use camels as freight animals to traverse the desert.

Backers of the scheme insisted that if camels could be used successfully in Africa and Asia, they might also flourish in the "Great American Desert".

Some 75 Mediterranean camels, along with Greek camel tenders, were imported in the mid-1850s and delivered to Camp Verde, Texas. The so-called "dromedary express" was underway.

One of the first tests of the camels was at Fort Tejon on top of the Grapevine Grade, south of Bakersfield.

The experiment didn't come without a fight. When Lt. Edward F. Beale was ordered by Secretary of War

John B. Floyd to pick up 25 camels from Camp Verde and take them to his command post in California, he exploded.

"What," he asked, "was an Army man going to do with a herd of camels?"

While Beale fumed, both orally and in written letters to Secretary Floyd, the secretary stood firm. Beale had no choice but to travel back to California with 25 camels in tow, along their Greek camel tenders.

The army found camels could carry heavy loads, but they were too slow to carry the U.S. mail.

The first contingent of camels made its initial experimental trip from Arizona in only fifteen days, with the camels swimming the Colorado River on their way.

On January 8, 1858, the population of Los Angeles turned out to witness the arrival of the state's first camel caravan as they arrived at Fort Tejon.

Despite Beale's initial displeasure, he found the camels reliable, docile, and patient. They would not stampede as the mules did.

Their biggest detriment was the need to tend them during stops to camp, as the camels would amble for miles in search of forage. But the trip across the desert to California changed Beale's thinking about the beasts. He came to like them.

The camels did suffer from the rocky soil of the Mojave desert, which chewed into their soft hooves. The Mojave was not the same as the soft sands of the eastern Mediterranean.

Even so, Beale took a liking to the usefulness of the camels and refused to return them to Camp Verde when asked by his superiors to do so.

His excuse was the camels would be invaluable should California become involved in a military action, such as a threatened war with the Mormons. Instead, he left the camels at the ranch of his business partner, Samuel A. Bishop, who operated a teamster service.

Bishop continued to use the camels to haul freight to his own ranch and to the developing town of Fort Tejon during the next year.

Mojave Indians often harassed teamsters along the route where Bishop hauled freight for Beale's work crews. The Indians willingly attacked civilians travelling through the area, but shunned soldiers.

At one point, Bishop's men encountered a large force of Mojaves. The Mojaves sent ominous signals of wanting to attack the teamsters. Bishop ordered his men to mount the camels and make a charge.

It is said this was the only "camel charge" in the west. Ironically, the Army, which owned the beasts, had nothing to do with it. The surprise charge did rout the Mojaves, however, who were unaccustomed to fighting men on such strange beasts.

Beale was eventually ordered to turn his camels over to the Army. He told his partner Bishop to take the camels to the Army at Fort Tejon.

The camels had been worked so hard and were in such poor physical shape they were not worth feeding. They were consequently moved to a rented grazing area 12 miles from the post.

As the animals' health returned, the Army resumed its experiments with camels. In one test, camel tenders were ordered to deliver mail by camel, much like the Pony Express. Mail was carried from Fort Tejon to Fort Mojave on the Colorado River.

In the first trial, the camel dropped dead from exhaustion at the Fishponds (now known as Daggett). A second attempt at "camel express" mail ended with the camel dying at Sugar Loaf (now Barstow). In each trial, the camel rider ended up stripping the mail pouch from the animal and carrying it by foot to Fort Mojave.

The Army eventually determined camels were no faster than the two-mule buckboard it had under contract to deliver mail to Fort Mojave. Camels, they found, were not express animals, even though they could haul heavy loads.

In another poorly organized and confusing experiment, the Army turned its camels over to a survey crew mapping the California-Nevada border.

The group became lost often, and never found the coordinates for the new Nevada-California border. As the survey crew floundered, drifting into the northern Mojave Desert, they soon lost their mules and abandoned their equipment.

The slow-plodding camels took the struggling crew over the Sierra to Visalia. The camels had saved the day.

Chapter 8

The Building of a Railroad

'The 'Big Four' were wily scoundrels'

Californians were abuzz about the building of a railroad that would link the Mississippi Valley with the Pacific Coast as early as 1826.

Twenty years later, George Wilkes, proposed the construction of a railroad across western America to the Pacific. It could be built, he said, with huge grants of public land stretching on either side of the right of way, all the way to the Pacific in Oregon.

The Pacific Railroad Survey Act of March 1853 authorized the United States Corps of Topographical Engineers to make surveys.

A chief promoter of such a railroad was Theodore Judah, an engineer, who came to California in 1854 to survey and supervise construction of the first railroad on the Pacific coast.

A year later, he completed a 20-mile short line that led out of Sacramento toward the placer country in the Sierras.

When large mineral deposits were discovered on the Comstock mine in Nevada in 1859, the building of an overland railroad out of Sacramento up through the Sierras became feasible. The line would travel down the eastern slopes to the vicinity of Virginia City.

When Judah attempted to interest San Francisco investors in such a project, he repeatedly came away empty-handed. He met skepticism everywhere until one night in 1860, when he persuaded a small group of merchants to meet above the hardware store of Huntington, Hopkins and Company in Sacramento.

Work on the last mile of The Pacific Railroad
(California State Library)

Most of the men attending were of moderate wealth. Judah emphasized the value of a railroad as a supply facility for the Comstock. His approach caught the interest of four men who were later destined to become "The Big Four" in California history.

Included were Leland Stanford, a wholesale grocer, Charles Crocker, a dry goods dealer, and Mark Hopkins and Collis P. Huntington, partners in a wholesale hardware establishment.

Before the evening was over, the four men had committed themselves to the purchase of stock. Stanford became president, Huntington, vice-president, and Hopkins, treasurer. The Central Pacific Railroad Company was formally incorporated in June, 1861.

Judah convinced Congress to pass the Pacific Railroad Act of 1862. The bill authorized a loan in the form of United States bonds to be issued at the rate of $16,000 per mile of track laid on level ground, $32,000 in the semi-mountainous land, and $48,000 per mile in the mountains.

The four investors wanted a road built quickly, regardless of quality, so they could start reaping profits. Judah, the engineer, was only interested in building a railroad that would meet an engineer's rigid standards.

He and the big four came to loggerheads over the construction standards the line would be built. The four disgruntled investors offered Judah a chance to buy them out.

Judah headed for New York. He was positive eastern investors would provide him with the necessary capital.

During the trip through the Panama Canal, Judah contracted a fever. He died from the malady, ultimately solving the problem of divided management for the "Big Four." The "Big Four" had complete control of the Central Pacific.

Labor was in short supply. Most available workers were employed by the booming Comstock mine in Virginia City, Nevada.

Crocker, now in charge of railroad construction, decided to experiment with Chinese labor. This proved so successful, Orientals were gathered up from hundreds of towns and hamlets in California. Additional Chinese labor was imported from Asia by a concern in which Crocker had an interest.

The Big Four had already completed a stranglehold on the Northern California Bay area. They had control of the Southern Pacific Railroad Company and they were chief owners of the Central Pacific. They were clearly planning to capture the rest of California.

When they merged the Southern Pacific with the Central Pacific, they guaranteed there would be no competition from another transcontinental line.

The Big Four envisioned a rail line that would go from San Francisco in the north to Los Angeles and San Diego in the south. The route would travel through the San Joaquin Valley.

They chose the San Joaquin Valley because the lands there were mostly government owned and more easily acquired than the private lands along the coast.

They brought all their influence to bear in obtaining rights of way through cities and towns. Los Angeles, the largest town in Southern California, owned a small rail connection to San Pedro and Santa Monica.

Charles Crocker threatened to leave Los Angeles off the main line of the Southern Pacific if the city fathers did not hand over ownership of the Los Angeles and San Pedro Railroad. In addition, the city would have to pay The Big Four a subsidy of $600,000 in the process.

The railroad powerhouse had already made San Bernardino an example of what could happen to towns resisting their wills. When San Bernardino balked at dealing with the Big Four, Southern Pacific built its division a few miles away, creating the railroad town of Colton.

There were other railroad spite towns, as well, including Lathrop, near Stockton, and Goshen, near Visalia.

Even with their vast power, the Big Four lost some battles. Collis P. Huntington attempted to change proposed harbor construction from San Pedro to Santa Monica. The railroad barons owned a stretch of oceanfront at Santa Monica.

The people of Los Angeles resisted. They feared continued domination by the railroad company if they didn't fight Huntington's proposal.

It took the collaborative efforts of the Los Angeles chamber of commerce, the L.A. Times, and a group of citizens that formed a "Free Harbor League" to combat the railroad tyrants.

Senator Stephen M. White joined in the battle to keep the proposed port in San Pedro. Even Joseph Pulitizer's newspaper, the New York World, opposed the move to Santa Monica as being "a special privilege".

In a clever tax move, the Big Four made Kentucky its legal corporate headquarters for the Southern Pacific, which now included all the property of the Central Pacific.

While they did not plan to operate from there, incorporation laws in Kentucky were among the most lax in the nation.

No railroad in any other region enjoyed such freedom from competition as did the Southern Pacific. The Big Four used its broad powers to adopt any system of freight rates they wanted to devise.

The railroad often favored one shipper, while at the same time, would put another one out of business with its confiscatory rates.

It wasn't unusual for railroad agents to demand a shipper allow them to examine his books before setting a shipping rate, generally set at what the agent determined the shipper was able to pay.

It was said that no railroad in the world brandished a greater variety of rates.

Chapter 9

A Strange Way to Measure Land

'Don Jose's measurements have withstood several court challenges.'

In appreciation of Jose Maria Verdugo's military service, California Governor Pedro Fages granted him the land known as Rancho San Rafael. This was a property that was very special to Don Jose. It was where he met his wife.

In a letter to Don Jose granting him retirement status, Governor Fages wrote, "You may retire to your rancho. But remember not to let your cattle graze on mission land. And treat the Indians kindly."

As it turned out, it was not Don Jose who intruded on mission lands, but quite the reverse. Verdugo found mission sheep grazing on his lands. Ditches for water were built by mission Indians, along with huts for the shepherds.

The sheep, Don Jose learned, belonged to Mission San Gabriel, which was under the supervision of a new padre, who did not know where Don Jose's land began and ended.

Horsemen use a fifty-yard rawhide lariat
to measure and map Don Jose Verdugo's property.
The measuring method has withstood court challenges.

This wasn't the only trouble for Don Jose. On the other side of the rancho, Don Jose found workers from Mission San Fernando harvesting crops on land that he owned.

Not knowing how to deal with the problem, Don Jose complained to the governor. "The missions are using my land, They are stealing my crops and altering my water."

The governor notified the alcalde in the pueblo of Los Angeles: "Go out to Rancho San Rafael and help Don Jose Maria Verdugo. His land is between two missions. Measure his land so that all will know which land is his."

This began a strange method of land measurement.

Don Jose, the alcalde, and two vaqueros went out to measure the land. The vaqueros brought with them a fifty-vara (about fifty yards) reata. On each end was tied a long stick.

One vaquero would hold his stick at the starting place, while the other galloped his horse until the reata was taut and straight, at which point he would place his stick in the ground. The other vaquero, in turn, then galloped with the reata to make another 50-yard measurement.

As the measuring progressed, Don Jose and the alcalde drew a map of the land. "We must be accurate," Don Jose told the alcalde. "It must stand against later claims."

The land was thus measured, mile after mile, 50 yards at a time. Don Jose was insistent on properly marking his lands so that his map would show exactly where his boundaries should be.

The preciseness of Don Jose's measurements have stood the test of time, and remain intact today. Other rancheros, which marked their property edges with a pile of stones that frequently disappeared, or by a creek bed, which later went dry, were not so lucky.

Eventually, the rancho was left to Don Jose's son, Julio, and to his daughter, Catalina. Don Julio was described as a flashy dresser who often galloped into the pueblo of Los Angeles with a black silk handkerchief over his head.

He wore a low-crowned hat with a wide brim. His jacket was of heavy black cloth, sometimes velvet, with rows of gold buttons and fancy stitches. His trousers were split to the knees at the side, with fancy stitches to match his coat.

When Don Julio would ride by, villagers would recall old Don Jose Maria Verdugo. "There goes old Don Jose's son, looking like his father," they would say.

Chapter 10

California's Spanish Place Names

'Few Spanish place names are pronounced correctly'

Thirty-two of California's 58 counties have Spanish names. Some others are Indian names and may be mistaken as Spanish because of their similarity. The towns and counties in California, came about their names in a variety of ways.

It doesn't take newcomers to California long to figure out the "j" in San Jose is really pronounced like an English "h".

Few Spanish place names are ever pronounced quite properly except by purists and Latinos. In their book, "California's Spanish Place Names," authors Barbara and Rudy Marinacci lay out the history surrounding the naming of communities up and down California.

"The history of a region is written in the ways people have used the land," explains the authors. "The names given to this land reflect the stages of its development."

When Americans surged into California in the late 1840s and early 1850s, the population jumped from

12,000 people to 100,000 in 1849 alone. It is ironic that this increase in population was brought on by the finding of the very gold that had eluded the early Spanish explorers.

Few Spanish place names are ever pronounced correctly.

Gaspar de Portola's expedition from San Diego to Monterey is considered the richest source of California place-names.

These explorers applied names to California's lakes, mountains, and locales. It was the trail Portola blazed through the wilderness stretching from San Diego Bay to San Francisco Bay that became the well-known "El Camino Real" (the Royal Road or the King's Highway).

Hundreds of California's existing place and street names are derivations from actual ranchos. Consider, for instance, Rodeo Drive, the penultimate residence of "los ricos" in Beverly Hills.

The street, which was named for the land grant, "Rancho Rodeo de las Aguas", does not refer to a cattle roundup at all, but to the "gathering" of waters from the streams of the Benedict and Coldwater canyons.

Some of the first California lands claimed by the Spanish empire were "concedos" or concessions awarded to soldiers who had served the province loyally, but were now aging or ailing and wished to retire.

Most of the 20 early land concessions became very important, both historically and economically. In accepting the grants, the landholders were expected to build a structure on the premises, to be used by vaquero caretakers, and to stock the rancho with several hundred cattle.

The rancheros themselves, however, were expected to dwell in the closest pueblo, a condition meant to increase a settlement's population and improve its caliber.

This live-in requirement was often ignored because of its inconvenience, though some families continued to keep a casa de pueblo as well as their casa de rancho.

Among some of the most notable of those first twenty land concessions was "Rancho San Rafael" or "La Zanja", which belonged to the Verdugos. It encompassed almost 40,000 acres. The cities of Glendale, Burbank, and Eagle Rock now sit on portions of that rancho.

The Verdugo name itself has perpetuated in mountains, a canyon, and a town named after it.

Rancho Santa Gertrudes or "Los Nietos" was originally owned by the Nieto family. Eventually, it was subdivided into five ranchos, including Los Cerritos and Los Alamitos.

It was a huge acreage that contained land between the San Gabriel and Santa Ana rivers and stretched from the mountains to the sea. Long Beach, Downey, and Norwalk all sit upon this property.

Rancho San Pedro, the Domingues estate, was a triangular section that is now covered by settlements such as Compton, Redondo Beach, and Wilmington

Nuestra Senora del Refugio, or "El Refugio", was conceded to Jose Francisco Ortega, who served as sergeant on the Portola expedition and is considered the first European to behold San Francisco Bay.

Rancho El Conejo lands straddle both Ventura and Los Angeles counties in the vicinity of Thousand Oaks. Conejo (rabbit) still appears there as a name for a mountain, a valley, and a creek.

El Encino was assigned to a soldier named Reyes in 1785. This concession was challenged by the padres at Mission San Fernando. They claimed the grant encroached upon the mission's lands and therefore interfered with the Indian's property rights.

The concession was withdrawn, but after mission secularization, a private ranch took the same title. The town of Encino was named after this rancho.

As Portola's soldiers marched inland from San Diego northward, they continued applying Spanish names along the way. When they camped near a lagoon in one small valley, they called it Canada de San Alejo (St. Alexius's Canyon). The spelling has since evolved into San Elijo Valley.

When the soldiers camped along a lake near what is now Arroyo Grande, they called it Laguna Larga (Long Lake). It is now known as Guadalupe Lake.

In one valley, where they killed a bear, they found the meat lean but delicious. Some of the men wanted to call the place Canada de las Viboras (Viper Canyon). The name that endured, however, is Oso Flaco (Lean Bear).

As the expedition neared the latitude given by Sebastian Vizcaino as Monterey Bay, the soldiers stayed close to the coast.

When they passed through an oak-studded area in what is now the Jolon area, they promptly named it Los Robles. It was letter selected as the site for a third mission, San Antonio de Padua.

Passing further along, friendly Indians approached, and Father Crespi heard the word "soledad" (solitude). This, he said, would be a suitable name for the place and its Indians. A mission established later carries the name, Nuestra Senora de la Soledad.

During the long march, Portolo's soldiers gave many of the place names that exist today in California.

Chapter 11

Cotton, Silkworms and Oranges

A variety of ventures flourished and failed

Few of the flurries of newcomers to California in search of gold in 1848 were prepared for the rigors that gold mining demanded.

When "gold fever" abated, these newcomers sought other opportunities that might provide them a path to riches. Some of the disappointed ones returned to their home states, but vast numbers remained in the west, more often California, and in particular, in San Francisco.

When gold was discovered, San Francisco claimed a population of only 812 persons. The town had two hotels and two wharves, neither of which was finished. San Francisco's population dropped very near to zero as everyone rushed to the mines.

San Francisco was close to becoming a ghost town, and probably would have if gold diggings had not started pouring in from the mines. With this new-found wealth, the town revived.

Miners wanted supplies, and San Franciscans were more than willing to supply them. In doing so,

San Francisco indeed proved a fine outlet for the miners gold.

Hotels and lodging houses were not above putting 10 or 20 men in a single room at which they extracted an exorbitant price.

There were booms and busts in a wide array of ventures, including great excitement in silkworm production. Newspapers and magazines were hailing the advantages of California as a silk producing center.

The culture of silkworms started in a small way, but soon developed into a first class boom. Millions of silkworms and silkworm eggs were imported from France and Japan, sometimes at ridiculous prices,. Large tracts of land were planted to mulberry trees, a prime food supply for silkworms.

This boom went bust about as quickly as it started. Yet, remnants of the silk movement remained for years in some areas, marked by rows of mulberry trees that had been planted to feed the silkworms.

The silk industry experiment, some historians say, was a venture that was doomed from the start.

One crop that did at first boom, then busted, and then boomed again was cotton. The development of irrigation brought on a growth in California agriculture that was unprecedented during the 1870 to 1890 era.

Some ranchers planted hundreds of acres of cotton. One farmer planted cotton on a large tract west of Figueroa Street in Los Angeles. Another company planted 10,000 acres of the fiber crop near Bakersfield.

The cotton plants yielded heavily, but the farmers had failed to allow for a very necessary element to growing cotton, labor.

The cotton would have to be harvested, but there were no pickers available to pick the white bolls from the vines. Cotton fields were allowed to become overgrown by grass and the cotton growers generally went into bankruptcy.

The early interest in cotton died out for a period, but years later farmers again experimented with cotton, eventually making California one of the world's major cotton producing areas of the world. Instead of human labor, machines now harvest the crop.

One real California success from the beginning was the planting of orange trees. The first oranges were planted at several of the Franciscan missions long before the coming of the Americans.

By 1875, there were a number of well-established orchards in Southern California from which as many as five million cartons of oranges were shipped each year to San Francisco.

These oranges, grown from seedlings, were quite different in both taste and appearance to the later-appearing Washington navel and Valencia varieties that now dominate California citrus orchards.

Indeed, it was the introduction of the Washington navel that brought about a major revolution in California horticulture. This introduction was spawned when a woman, who lived in Bahia, Brazil, sent 12 small orange trees to her friend, the Commissioner of Agriculture in Washington, D.C.

Three of these trees were shipped to Mr. and Mrs. L.C. Tibbetts, in Riverside, California, who planted them near their home. Some reports claim it was Mrs.

Tibbetts who dashed the trees with her daily dishwater, which played a major role in keeping the three trees alive and healthy.

This daily irrigation and perhaps whatever nutrients were available in the dishwater, kept the orange trees growing well.

When the trees reached maturity, buds were taken from them and grafted onto seedling rootstock. The Washington Navel eventually became the most popular orange in the U.S.

One of those three original trees shipped to Riverside still stands as a national monument. It is fenced in to preserve the tree and protect its buds from poachers.

Chapter 12

The California Presidios

San Francisco saluted with borrowed gunpowder

When visiting Russians arrived in San Francisco, soldiers at the presidio, the most important of the California forts, were thrown into an embarrassing situation.

Their armory was so poorly stocked, they had to borrow gunpowder from the Russian visitors to return a proper salute.

This was not the only embarrassment of the military personnel manning these installations. Even the officers, the aristocracy of these frontier fortresses, lived under primitive conditions, making them the pity of foreign visitors.

Spanish friars were diligent in keeping settlers, and especially the soldiers, away from their new converts, the Indians. Soldiers were too apt to take advantage of the mission's charges, especially the women.

Presidios, with their small troops of soldiers, were consequently located at remote distances from both the missions and from the pueblos.

California was divided into four military districts, with a presidio in each one.

These fortresses, established at San Diego, Monterey, San Francisco, and Santa Barbara, were intended to protect the missions from Indians and intruders, and to guard Spanish claims to the area from foreign aggression.

But the presidios were so poorly financed and maintained, they generally fell into decay.

Soldiers were poorly outfitted. To their disgust, they were more often used to perform menial tasks rather than military duties. They were used to erect buildings, care for flocks and herds, and even more to their distaste, cultivate and tend the soil.

The soldiers did learn to be enterprising. They would employ Indians to do their menial tasks. In exchange for their labors, Indians might receive a string of beads, a dish of porridge, a pair of cast-off shoes, or a bit of cloth.

Presidios were located at strategic positions, often at the entrances of the best ports. Small groups of houses, inhabited by settlers, traders, and families of the soldiers grew up around the presidios.

While the Spanish government may have been lax in fortifying its presidios, it was precise in planning down to the minutest detail the layout of its pueblos in Spanish America.

The inducements offered to attract residents to these new communities attracted more low life criminals than it did upstanding settlers. Mexicans emptied their jails in Sinaloa and Sonora, sending their riff-raff northward.

Pueblo Architecture

The Spanish pueblo planners were precise. Before a pueblo was located, it was first determined if adequate water was available. There must be wood for both building and for fuel, and sufficient arable land and pasture for livestock to maintain the pueblo's populace. A great requirement was the proper soil for the building of adobe structures.

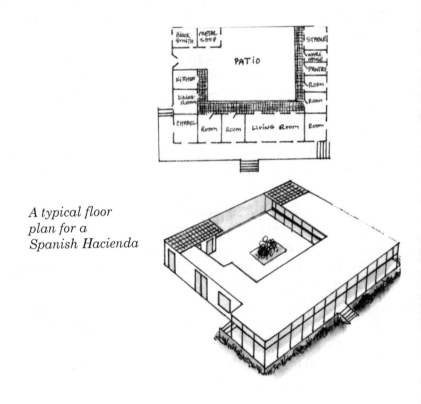

A typical floor plan for a Spanish Hacienda

While the designers of the pueblos were exact, the towns in Alta California were much alike. A plaza was the center of town, for that's where the people met, shopped, and held their celebrations. Around the plaza were grouped the church, the town hall, and other important buildings.

To induce colonists to come to the new province, Spanish authorities provided many incentives. Each new settler received a house lot, a parcel for farming, and use of the common pastureland.

Settlers received a small subsidy of $10 per month for the first two years, and $5 a month for the next three years. They were exempted from taxes during this first 5-year period.

The Spanish government's grandiose plans did not work. Those most ill-suited to colonize came forth. Many recruits to the new pueblos were deep-dyed criminals.

In spite of generous government support and elaborate planning, the pueblos of Alta California never really prospered. Those settlers that came were poorly trained for becoming frontiersmen and more inclined to find ways to exploit the Indians than to do the labor themselves.

Private ranchos were not originally intended as a means to settle California. Scattered ranchos were considered hard to defend and control, and the authorities discouraged them.

There were some land grants made for political reasons, or for personal friendship, and to military men, especially, in remuneration for services. The first rancheros in California were Spanish soldiers. Many had come to California with the explorers.

The result was the granting of only some 25 ranchos and the creation of the landed elite.

These early grants formed the basis of the extensive rancho system that dominated society when Spanish sovereignty ended in Alta California in 1821. While the sovereignty ended, Spanish institutions remained.

About 40 years after Spain had started her colonies in California, Mexico became independent from Spain and claimed California as her own. In 1825, Spain relinquished its rule, and the Mexican flag flew over Monterey, the Capital.

Chapter 13

The Whipping Boys

'The driver was the boss'

Not everyone could manage a stagecoach. The stagecoach driver was held in higher esteem when on the summit of the Sierra than was the millionaire statesman who might be riding beside him.

While most stage drivers were sober, at least while on duty, nearly all were fond of an occasional "eye opener". A good driver was the captain of his craft. He was feared by his timid passengers, awed by stableboys, and was the trusty agent of his employer.

The seat next to the driver, weather permitting, was the preferred seat of the men passengers. But this was one seat that was reserved, and it was not gotten by simply being the first to hop on the left front wheel rim and climbing into the box.

If the driver didn't want the person who took the seat there, he would firmly order him down, and then enjoy the passenger's discomfiture for the next ten miles.

To sit in the driver's seat, one proceeded very much in the manner of securing an appointment to a high office. He went to the source of authority---above the driver himself---to the superintendent and even to the president of the company.

Carpinteria was always a welcome rest spot for passengers on Charlie Parkhurst's run. For one thing, Shepard's Inn, run by a former Iowa farmer, James Erwin Shepard, had wonderful food, good beds, and pleasant hospitality.

Charlie Parkharst was a respected
stage driver who hid his secret for years.

In the shantytown of Los Angeles, there was little to attract travelers, although they could purchase ice cream and hot tomales there.

Charlie Parkhurst was one of the more skillful stagecoach drivers, not only in California, but throughout the west. He was variously called "One-eyed" or "Cockeyed" Charlie, because he had lost an eye when kicked by a horse. For 20 years, he drove stagecoach in California.

Twice Charlie was held up. The first time, he was forced to throw down his strongbox because he was unarmed. The second time, he was prepared.

When a road agent ordered the stage to stop and commanded Charlie to throw down its strongbox, Parkhurst leveled a shotgun blast into the chest of the outlaw, whipped his horses into a full gallop, and left the bandit in the road.

One-eyed Charlie was known as one of the toughest, roughest, and the most daring of stagecoach drivers. Like most drivers, he was proud of his skill in the extremely difficult job as "whip". Proper handling of the horses and the great coaches was an art that required much practice, experience, and not the least, courage.

Whips received high salaries for the times, sometimes as much as $125 a month, plus room and board.

"How in the world can you see your way through this dust?" one passenger asked Charlie.

"Smell it. Fact is," Charlie replied, "I've traveled over these mountains so often I can tell where the road is by the sound of the wheels. When they rattle, I'm on hard ground; when they don't rattle I gen'r'lly look over the side to see where she's agoing."

Yet, little was really known about Charlie Parkhurst before or after he came to California. It wasn't until his body was prepared for burial that his true secret was discovered.

Charlotte "Charlie" Parkhurst was a woman. One doctor claimed that at some point in her life, she had been a mother.

Unknowingly, Parkhurst could claim a national first. After voting on Election Day, November 3, 1868, Charlie was probably the first woman to cast a ballot in any election. It wasn't until 52 years later that the right to vote was guaranteed to women by the nineteenth amendment.

All stagecoach drivers, including Charlie, considered their whips worth their weight in gold. The whips were a badge of honor for the good stagecoach driver.

Some drivers would as soon be caught without their pants as without their whips. Many of the whips used by the stage drivers were fine works of art, generally ornamented with handcrafted silver ferules girdling a handle made of hickory. Many of these whips are prized museum pieces today.

Selin Carrillo was the last surviving stagecoach driver in Santa Barbara County, driving daily over the San Marcos Pass. He disdained the image of stagecoach drivers as presented by Hollywood, who he said probably couldn't even use a whip if they carried one at all.

Whips were never sold, loaned, borrowed, or traded. In his book, "Stagecoach Days in Santa Barbara County", Walker A. Tompkins wrote, "Whips were considered a part of the driver, who kept the lashes well-oiled and as pliable as "a snake in the sun."

Most stagecoach whips had buckskin lashes, usually from 11 to 12 feet in length, attached to a five-foot hickory shaft. The lashes were 10 feet too short to reach the lead team, which was controlled by reining. Some rare drivers did carry a "six-horse whip" with a 22-foot lash, but these were mainly for circus and rodeo appearances, and considered too unwieldy for practical use.

The driver took his whip with him when off duty, and always hung it up. He never rested it in a corner for fear of warping the stock. Neither did he wrap the lash around the handle for fear of curling the thongs.

Some stagecoach drivers were truly adept horsemen and could control three spans of fast-moving horses with a double fistful of leather ribbons. Carrillo especially deplored the movie directors who forced their stages to travel at a full gallop, up hill and down, day in and day out.

Neither did stagecoach drivers do a lot of whip cracking as depicted in the movies. Cracking of the whip was used sparingly by the top-grade stagecoach drivers.

These drivers were concerned that the pistol-shot reports made by the whips would only startle their passengers out of their naps or, worse yet, spook their teams.

More often, good drivers would use the whips to give light attention-getting flicks to a "wheeler's" rump or wake up the swing (middle) span of horses.

Roads had to be built at public expense before stagecoaches were given a route. Some were little more than ox-cart tracks linking the various ranchos.

Even the El Camino Real, the storied "King's Highway" was little more than a foot trail.

Stage routes sometimes crossed fenced cattle range. On some ranchos, the owners built gates to prevent cattle from straying. Grace Davison, the late Santa Barbara County historian of Ballard, recalled one driver resented getting out and closing the gate.

He warned the ranch owner that his stage was carrying United States Mail and if he found the gate closed the next time the mail came through he would take "stern measures".

The next day, when he found the gate shut, the driver dismounted, took an axe he had brought along for just such an occasion, and made a pile of kindling of the gate.

No action was taken by the rancher, except for the fact that he had a new gate built which could be opened and closed by a person on the driver's seat.

A tale is told about stage driver Whispering George Cooper. He got his name because of his loud bellow, which could be heard for miles against a wind while he pushed his team up a treacherous pass.

At one point, Whispering George needed to repair a broken single tree that had developed a bad split. He scoured the stage for a bit of rope or a scrap of baling wire, to make the repair. At that moment, his team was spooked by a rattlesnake slithering across the road in front of them.

George killed the snake, measuring five feet or more in length. A passenger commented how much the snake resembled a rope.

"By gawd, that's what I'll use it for!" exclaimed George. He wrapped the dead snake around the single tree and knotted it into place. It worked, holding the damaged single tree together until it reached a relay station.

The term "stagecoach" came about in medieval Europe, when public coach travel was the only way one could get from one point to another without walking.

Trips were generally made in easy stages because of bad roads and the lack of overnight lodgings along the way. Hence, the term "stage" coach.

Ten Commandments for Stage Passengers

The following rules were among those posted at stage stations and sometimes on the ceiling of the stagecoach itself.

1. Abstainance from liquor is preferred. If you must drink, share the bottle. To do otherwise makes you appear selfish. And don't overlook the driver.

2. If ladies are present, gentlemen are urged to forego smoking cigars and pipes, as the odor of same is repugnant to the weaker sex. Chewing tobacco is permitted, if you spit WITH the wind, not against it.

3. Gentlemen passengers must refrain from the use of rough language in the presence of ladies and children. This rule does not apply to the driver, whose team may not be able to understand genteel language.

4. Robes are provided for your comfort during cold or wet weather. Hogging robes will not be tolerated. The offender will be obliged to ride outside with the driver.

5. Snoring is disgusting. If you sleep, sleep quietly.

6. Don't use your fellow passenger's shoulder for a pillow. He or she may not understand, and friction could result.

7. Firearms may be kept on your person, for use in emergencies. Do not discharge them for pleasure, or shoot at wild animals along the roadsides. The noise riles the horses.

8. In the event of a runaway, remain calm. Jumping from the coach may kill you, leave you injured or at the mercy of the elements, highwaymen and coyotes.

9. Topics of discussion to be avoided have to do with religion, politics, and above all, stagecoach robbery and accidents.

10. Gentlemen guilty of unchivalrous behavior toward lady passengers will be put off the stage. It is a long walk back to Santa Barbara. A word to the wise is sufficient.

Chapter 14

A Man Named Hollister

'His Name is emblazoned on two counties'

It is doubtful that William Welles Hollister could envision the mark he would make on California after driving 6,000 head of sheep from Licking County, Ohio, to California.

Hollister's 2,000-mile trek, on which a brother, a sister, and 50 herdsmen accompanied him, ended in what is now San Juan Bautista.

When he arrived, only 1,000 of his original 6,000 sheep were alive. Still, he parlayed what was left of this Ohio wool on-the-hoof into one of California's great private fortunes.

He is responsible for colonizing the town of Hollister in San Benito County and Lompoc in Santa Barbara County.

"Because so many California towns are named for saints," said one of the town organizers of Hollister, "let's name this one for a sinner."

Hollister was an industrious person. His fortune swelled during the next 14 years. He sold his San Justo Rancho in San Benito County to move back to the Santa Barbara country that he admired so while driving his band of scraggly sheep up the coast.

Colonel Hollister, in partnership with the Dibblee Brothers, Thomas and Albert, seized every opportunity to purchase land grants. They bought the Refugio Rancho in Santa Barbara County, along with several other land grants, including the Lompoco, Las Cruces, Salsipuedes, San Julian, and Mission Viejo.

Hollister's main desire was to acquire the Tecolotito Canyon area on the Dos Pueblos grant, which he had coveted 17 years before on his sheep drive.

The property was on the market, but it had a cloudy title. The minor heirs of the original grant holder were still alive and there was a question of whether the property could be sold. This didn't deter Hollister from plunging ahead with the deal. The legality of the purchase was still in litigation when he died.

Money was of little consequence to the now-wealthy Hollister. He built more than six miles of fencing, virtually unheard of in Santa Barbara County. He established a dairy herd and imported a landscape gardener to plant velvety lawns and exotic flora around the property.

He widened the county road, now Hollister Avenue, linking Santa Barbara and Goleta, and bordered it with an avenue of palms and pines.

Always adventurous, Hollister imported 25 bushels of Japanese tea plants, which he thought would grow in the soil and climate of his Dos Pueblos Rancho.

He hired two Japanese tea planters to plant his 50,000 seedlings. A frost killed the entire tea project overnight.

The Refugio Rancho is probably the first working cattle ranch apart from mission operation in Santa Barbara County. Hollister and the Dibblee brothers purchased the property from the heirs of Capt. Jose Francisco de Ortega, who acquired the grant in 1834.

Spanish vaqueros placed the fresh hide of a slaughtered steer over a bush. The smell of the bloody hide drew wild cattle out off the brush like a magnet.

James J. Hollister, Sr., a son of Col. Hollister, supervised Rancho Refugio, running it in a style not unlike the "Old West". He was known for employing the "bloody hide" method of drawing stray critters from the chaparral-choked canyons on the ranch.

It was a method supposedly invented by the Ortegas and involved the placement of a hide from a freshly butchered bull over a bush. The odor of the fresh hide drew bellowing cattle like a magnet from the brushy hillsides without the need of vaqueros.

Gov. Juan B. Alvarado granted 13 major ranches in Santa Barbara County between 1836 and 1842. The first grant bearing Alvarado's signature was La Punta de la Conception, a 24,992 acre tract. It was later divided into two better-known ranches, La Espada and El Cojo.

These names, meaning "the sword" and "the lame man" were dubbed on the properties by soldiers of the Portola Land Expedition that passed up the coast in 1769 in search of the ensenada of Monterey.

Chapter 15

The Medicine Men

'An 'Ill-Suited' Profession'

Being a tribal medicine man was a dangerous post. It was more-often an unwanted designation than a desired position.

It is unclear how individuals were selected for this singular honor, but it was usually done early in an Indian's young life. The young medicine man wasn't expected to use what questionable medical skills he might have until he grew older.

Many of those selected resented being given such responsibilities. As soon as his ministrations had sent a sufficient number---usually three---to the happy hunting grounds, the medicine man was no longer be deemed worthy of his position.

The Piute Indians required a higher standard of medical success from its medicine men than did most tribes. Any Piute healer who lost three patients in a short time would wisely arrange his affairs immediately. He would be marked for early and unceremonious removal.

Stones, arrows, lassos, in daylight and dark, were used to reduce the number of medicine men in active service.

Even if a patient did survive, it didn't always bode well for the medicine man, especially if the medicine man had predicted death at the time he was called.

If the patient got well, the tribal healer had made a "bad guess". His prediction was marked as a failure of prophecy, signifying that the medicine man did not know his business.

At the same time, if a medicine man predicted death for a patient, and the patient lived, the medicine man was still charged with losing the case.

Even the family, especially female relatives, of an unsuccessful medicine man were subject to ridicule.

These women were looked upon as witches, and were often the subjects of cold blooded murders. As late as 1886, there were instances of killing of both doctors and witches.

In later years, sick Indians more often requested treatment by a white physician than by their tribal medicine man.

Still, as late as 1916, an eerie tribal incantation was used to treat one of the Indian maidens of the Piute tribe. When the patient did not respond, a white doctor was called, but to no avail. The patient still died.

Most medicine men rituals were meant to drive away the demons possessing an individual. Indian sweathouses were used for patients with skin rashes. The sufferer went into a wickiup equipped with heating accessories, and after the temperature reached the desired degree, the patient would dash out and plunge into a cold stream of water.

"Make 'um sick man sit on ant's nest," was one rheumatism cure passed down in Indian lore. "Bimeby (by and by) heap holler---purty good. Mebbe so git well," the prescription read.

Euthanasia was practiced among some tribes. This practice was used on those who had grown old and were considered in the way. This person would be taken to some lone spot and left with a supply of food and water to die.

Some of the ancient Indians supervised their own death arrangements. Such was the case of Malarango, chief of the Coso Piutes, said to be 90 years or more and suffering from a host of ailments. He was left at the edge of a spring with a supply of pine nuts. His demise was anticipated to occur in three days.

It is noted that Indians of that time were without standards of time, and therefore not able to know their own ages. Their stories of the past are usually dated "a long time ago," even when referencing a period only two generations back.

The home of a dead person was generally burned, along with some part of his personal possessions. However little evidence has been found during excavations of old Indian gravesites that anything of real value was buried with the body.

Indian legend was often distorted way beyond the actual happening. For instance, a flood of purely local proportions may become all-enveloping, in narrations in later years.

Chapter 16

The Lost Woman of San Nicolas

'She was a female Robinson Crusoe'

San Nicolas is a windswept island about 65 miles from the nearest point on the California mainland. Ships carrying Aleut Indian hunters came to the island, bent on taking the valuable sea otters abounding at San Nicolas Island.

The island, only 8-miles long and 3-miles wide, is said to have been inhabited by a superior race of almost white Indians, most likely the blended offspring of trading ship sailors and the native Indians.

The Russian otter hunters were as attracted by the women on the island, and considered them as desirable for taking, as the sea otters. These villainous plunderers readily killed the male Indians who tried to defend their women

The remaining Indians on San Nicolas wrested a precarious living from the kelp beds surrounding the island. .

In 1835, the tiny tribe was so decimated that the Mexican government decided to move the Indians to Mission San Gabriel for protection as well as to save their pagan souls.

Not only had the sea otter population at San Nicolas been reduced to minimal numbers, but the Indian tribe itself had dwindled to a puny population of inhabitants.

One of the rescue vessels was the Peor es Nada, a schooner built by Joaquin Gomez in Santa Barbara. The name itself, which means, when loosely translated, "Better Than Nothing", perhaps indicates the builder's opinion of his finished product.

The little schooner was directed to San Nicolas Island to pick up the remnants of the island's residents. Because of an ominous storm brewing, the Peor es Nada quickly left the island, but not before one woman found that her baby was not aboard the schooner. The frantic mother leaped overboard and swam ashore to search for her child.

The captain of the schooner, one Charles Hubbard, decided the storm was too threatening to wait for the woman, and hastened to San Pedro, distributing its load of Indians among the various missions. The woman who had jumped overboard to search for her child was all but forgotten although three attempts were made to find her during the next 18 years.

It was in 1853 that Captain George Nidever decided to comb the island in search of the woman. When Nidever stepped ashore, he spotted a faint, yet fresh, footprint in the hard sand. He found other prints moving away from the sea toward steep cliffs that sheltered a cove.

Before he could trace the footprints up the cliff, a furious blast of a northwest wind sent the captain's schooner reeling. It was heeled over, tugging at its anchor, forcing the captain and crew to board and sail away from the island before the ship was wrecked against the rocks.

Sea otters attracted foreign hunters to San Nicholas Island in search of the valuable pelts.

A year later, Captain Nidever returned, determined to find the lost woman. He was accompanied by Carl Dittman, who later wrote an account of the trip.

Dittman's account, written in 1878, noted he and Nidever discovered a basket, woven of grass, placed in the a clump of high bushes.

The basket's contents included a dress or gown made of the skin of the shag. There were several skins of the same kind, cut in a square shape. The basket also held bone needles and knives; fishhooks made of abalone shell; and a rope made of sinews, about one-half inch in diameter and fully 25 feet long.

Dittman wrote, "This sinew rope was twisted as evenly as the best rope I have ever seen. I think that it was used in snaring seals, by making a noose and spreading it on the rocks near the beach where the seals were accustomed to sleep."

After Nidever and Dittman examined the items, Nidever suggested leaving the items strewn on the ground rather than replacing them in the basket.

In this way, when they returned and found the items had been replaced in the basket, they would know if the woman were still alive.

On another trip, Nidever and Dittman returned to the island and searched the beach for signs of the lost woman. Back from the beach and about two miles apart, Dittman found three small circular enclosures, made of sagebrush with thin walls about five feet high.

> *Outside and around each hut, they found several poles stuck in the ground, standing upright. Atop each pole were pieces of seal blubber, left there to dry.*

The Indian woman was discovered in a small enclosure on the mountainside. According to Dittman's report, she was seated cross-legged, engaged in separating the blubber from a piece of sealskin.

Dittman signaled other members of the crew, by raising his hat on a stick so as not alarm the woman, to join him. The crew surrounded the woman to prevent any escape.

She, however, made no effort to flee. Instead, she flashed a smile and bowed, chattering away in a language unintelligible to any, even the Indians.

The woman was no longer young and her head was covered with thick, matted hair. Her only companions were five wild dogs.

The men convinced the woman, with signs, to accompany them. She placed her things into a basket. These possessions included seal meat, which had become rank, and a seal's head from which putrefied brains oozed.

As the group arrived at a spring issuing from a shelf of rock, the woman stopped to wash. When they reached the boat, the woman crept forward to the bow, where she knelt, holding firmly to either side of the craft.

Following dinner, which the woman ate heartily, Dittman made a petticoat and a man's shirt for her from ticking. She asked Dittman to allow her to sew.

Nidever provided her with an old cloak that was almost in ribbons. Dittman had to thread the needle for her as her eyes seemed weak. She sewed up every rent and hole in the cloak. Her manner of sewing was peculiar. She placed her work across her knee, and thrust the needle through the cloth with the right hand and pulled the thread taut with the left.

She was taken to Santa Barbara and christened Juana Maria. The remarkable woman, who survived the rigors of the forlorn island, had lost the knowledge of language. She could impart her history only with signs and gestures.

While she received the best of care, the woman who had been lost so long, and who was the last human inhabitant of San Nicolas, became ill from eating too much fruit.

She lived only six weeks. Her story, however, is even more sensational than that of Robinson Crusoe, especially since his was fiction, and hers was not.

Chapter 17

The Post Office Tree

'Cowboys read their mail from the saddle'

A lone buttonwillow tree stands at the edge of town, a symbol for which the town of Buttonwillow was named. What is not widely known is that the tree once served as a cowboy post office.

Historians report the tree was so strategically located that passing cowboys would place messages in tin cans and hang them on the tree.

Such messages would read "Gone to Dobe Holes", "Meet us at Fowler", or "Left early for 10 field". It is believed the messages were more generally read from the saddle than from the ground.

The statement, "I'll meet you at the Buttonwillow," became a common one. Historians note the tree was originally a meeting place for the now extinct Tuhohe tribe of Yokuts Indians, who called the place Hahlu, which means buttonwillow.

Buttonwillow history dates back to the late 1800's, when California cattle barons Miller & Lux, the railroad magnates, and others bought government land at bargain prices.

Miller and Lux reportedly received land from the government for 25 cents an acre under the reclamation program then in effect.

The area was marsh and swamp land. A provision in the law required the buyer of such swamp land to survey the property in a boat. Henry Miller surveyed his property during the dry season. He sat comfortably in boat carried in a horse-drawn wagon.

Cowboys read their mail from their saddles.

Miller established a commissary and trading center near the buttonwillow tree. For a long time, cattle kept nibbling at the tree so Miller built a fence around it.

Some accounts say that Miller fenced the tree to provide shade for chickens that he kept inside the fence. Miller, historians claim, needed chickens to supply his hungry cowhands, chickens need shade, so the buttonwillow tree was used.

The following two stories about Henry Miller were told directly to the author by a former Miller and Lux employee.

Miller had some rather ingenious hiring practices when taking on new cowboys and ranch workers. During a job interview, Miller would ask the job seeker for his pocket knife. If the applicant did not have a knife, he was immediately dismissed. Miller contended a knife was a necessary part of a cowhand's gear.

A second tale concerns a pile of wood Miller always kept near a fence in the ranch yard. A job applicant would be directed to throw the pile of wood over the fence.

When that chore was finished, Miller would direct him to throw it back to its original side. If the worker refused, he was hired. If he complied, and threw the wood back to its original side, he was dismissed, apparently failing Henry Miller's I.Q. test.

The buttonwillow tree is still standing, and was dedicated a California State Landmark No. 492 on Feb. 24, 1952.

Chapter 18

The Chinese Are Coming

'These immigrants were harassed from day they arrived.'

When the ship "Eagle" docked in San Francisco in 1848, it carried the first Chinese immigrants to California, two men and a woman.

The two men went to work in the gold mines while the woman worked as a domestic for a family that had lived in China. These early immigrants led the way for the arrival of more than seven hundred Chinese in 1849.

By 1852, there were eighteen thousand Chinese men and only fourteen Chinese women in the state. This number would grow to 116,000 during the next fourteen years.

Some of the Chinese began working the abandoned placer mines of the Anglo miners, contenting themselves with less than half the return the original miners received. Their persistence and hard work brought about the wrath of the white miner population.

There were many that feared the industriousness of the Chinese immigrants, and it led to a great deal of prejudice in some quarters. These odd-appearing people from the Far East were considered "barbarians" who were encroaching on American territory.

One lawmaker introduced a measure that would have confined the Chinese to jobs as apprentices, but without success.

This didn't stop lawmakers from trying again, in

A popular slogan during this period as one that merchants used to headline their advertisements.

"The Chinese Must Go"

One saloon keeper wrote:
"His drinks are A-1 and his prices are low,
His motto is always, 'The Chinese Must Go!'
So call on your friends, workingmen, if you please,
Take a good solid drink and drive out the Chinese!"

1854, to impose a tax on any Asiatic landing in California.

The state Supreme Court struck down the tax, which was established at $50 per head, as unconstitutional.

Undaunted, the legislature then imposed, in 1854, foreign miner tax of six dollars a month. This tax was soon raised to eight dollars, and then again to ten dollars.

Legislators then enacted a law that excluded the testimony of a person of Chinese descent from testifying in any court case involving an Anglo.

The Chinese situation presented Californians with a dilemma. If the Asians were driven from the mines, it would mean a loss of thousands of dollars in miners' taxes. To leave them in the mines meant, assuredly, an increase in racial violence.

There was fear, too, that driving them from the mines would cause stress in other areas. For instance, the Chinese would leave the mines only to go into towns and agricultural districts where they would work for the barest wage, undercutting other workmen.

In exasperation, state lawmakers, in 1858, passed a law forbidding any more Chinese being brought into California. If a ship's captain were convicted of disobeying this order, he would be liable to a fine of $400 to $600 dollars, or imprisonment for up to one year.

A catch-all tax was enacted in 1862. This was a police tax amounting to $2.50 a month, which was to be levied on any Chinese male eighteen years of age or older not subject to the miners' tax.

This tax was declared unconstitutional by the supreme court. The court did uphold the law excluding Chinese testimony in court as legal, however.

So hostile was the racial environment in the 1860s that students of Chinese, Blacks or Indians could be barred from public schools. The law did allow for separate schools to be provided.

This law was modified in 1866 to read that Chinese students could be admitted to schools, if there were no objections by white parents.

Chinese immigrants provided important labor for a number of industries in the building of California, not the least of which was the railroads. Charles Crocker, construction boss for the Central Pacific, scoured the state for Chinese workers.

The need for more railroad workers resulted in the Pacific Mail Steamship Line bringing more workers directly from China. At one time, there was an estimated ten thousand to fifteen thousand Chinese laborers working on the railroad in California.

When the railroad was finished, Chinese laborers inundated San Francisco in 1870, flooding the labor market there. They were willing to work at any job for virtually any pay.

Again, the eager legislature stepped in and passed a law that would provide a fine of $1,000 to $5,000 on anyone bringing Chinese or Japanese nationals into California who could not provide evidence of the person's good character. This law, too, was declared unconstitutional.

The court's ruling did not deter the city council of San Francisco, however. This body passed an ordinance that prohibited any Chinese or Japanese from working on municipal public works.

Other counties joined the fray. Irrigation companies, by 1876, were expressly forbidden to use any Chinese workers on projects in Alameda, Contra Costa, Santa Clara, Stanislaus, Merced, Fresno, and Tulare counties.

There were many other instances of abuse against the Chinese population. San Francisco enacted a city rental ordinance calling for a fine of ten to fifty dollars per person if a space of less than five hundred feet per occupant was not available. The law was upheld in court.

Another ordinance required any male Chinese prisoner convicted of crimes in the city to have his hair cut within one inch of his head. This was said to be a greater indignity for the Chinese male than having his ears cropped. The mayor mercifully vetoed the law as being unnecessary---and barbarous.

Chapter 19

The Flour Sale

'Supporting the sanitary commission'

When the Civil War broke out, there were many Southerners in California. Many of these Southerners left California to join the Confederate forces.

In California, a strong Union party generally opposed the southerners, and it represented the majority of the people in California.

California's interest in the war was expressed in great part by its contributions to the Sanitary Commission. This was an organization set up to care for the sick and wounded in the Union armies, similar to today's Red Cross.

Californians donations to the Sanitary Commission are said to have totaled at least a million dollars, representing as much as one-fifth of the contributions the Commission received from all of the United States.

One of the major fund raising campaigns involved a sack of flour. In Austin, Nevada, a man named Gridley lost a political bet and auctioned off a sack of flour for the benefit of the wounded Civil War soldiers. The flour sold for $550.

The buyer agreed to let the same sack of flour be auctioned off in a neighboring town, where it was repeated a number of times before arriving in California. The sack of flour was sold in San Francisco, Sacramento, and any number of other towns.

Bids on the sack of flour sometimes ran as high as $3,000. By the end of the Civil War, this single sack of flour had amassed some $275,000 for the Sanitary Commission.

Chapter 20

The Governor and His Lady

'She was a beautiful hellion'

Pedro Fages came to Monterey in 1782 as California's new governor. He was at first unable to persuade his wife, Dona Eulalia, to accompany him. She wanted nothing to do with such a primitive country.

Eventually he convinced the lovely Eulalia the country was not near so barbaric as she imagined and she agreed to venture north. Fages met her in Loreto and the two made the long journey to Monterey.

During the trip, the governor and his lady were continually honored by a number of receptions, undoubtedly cheering her somewhat, and raising her expectations.

Not only was Eulalia the wife of the new governor, but she was also the first lady of high rank to visit the province.

Still the fiery Dona Eulalia was shocked at the poor conditions she found in Monterey. She deplored the naked Indians. She impulsively gave away her own clothes, as well as those of her husband, to those she deemed more needy.

It took the chiding of her husband to make her realize she could not readily replace her wardrobe. There were simply no shops in Alta California.

After the birth of her daughter in 1784, Dona Eulalia announced that she had had enough of this new land. She was unable to convince Don Pedro Fages, however, to let her pack herself and her children off to New Spain (Mexico) where she could enjoy a better standard of living.

Dona Eulalia decided to use stronger measures to get her way. She banned Don Pedro from her bedroom, making him keep his distance for three months. Fages was unfazed by the treatment.

This convinced Eulalia that her husband must be consorting with the servant girl he had picked up from friendly Indians of the Colorado.

In a rage, Eulalia confronted Fages, accusing him of adultery. Not satisfied, she charged into the streets where she told anybody who would listen about her husband's supposed infidelity, announcing loudly that she would seek a divorce.

While the friars attempted to console her, they still maintained she had no grounds for divorce. In no uncertain terms, Eulalia let it be known that she would go to the "infierno" (Hell) before she would go back to Fages. The friars ordered Dona Eulalia to stay at home in seclusion and do no more talking of her supposed plight.

Governor Fages, at this time, needed to fulfill a gubernatorial duty by making a trip to the south. He asked Father Noriega at Mission San Carlos to take care of Dona Eulalia while he was gone. He feared for her mental health.

Eulalia refused to go to the mission, locking herself and her children inside her room. Finally, Governor Fages showed his temper. He broke down Eulalia's bedroom door and threatened to tie her up and transport her to the mission himself. She relented and agreed to go on her own.

Still, she rampaged at the mission, causing the friars as much grief as possible, even creating great disturbances in church. The impatient friars once threatened to flog her and put her in chains if she didn't behave.

The quarrel between the Governor and his lady continued for another year before they again were reconciled, although it was not the last of Dona Eulalia's attempts to leave Monterey.

Soon after the reconcilation, and unknown to her husband, Eulalia wrote to the "Audiencia" of Guadalajara, asking that Fages be removed on the grounds of ill-health.

When Governor Fages learned what his wife had done, he headed off the communication.

Dona Eulalia eventually won out, nevertheless. Early in 1790, Fages himself asked to be relieved of his gubernatorial post. His petition was granted, and Dona Eulalia wasted little time in taking her children aboard the San Blas boat.

Fages had been told he need not await the arrival of a successor. Still, he stayed on another year, at which time he presumably joined his family in Mexico City. Fages is reported to have died in 1796.

Chapter 21

Political Corruption in Los Angeles

'Money could buy police and politicians'

Police often looked the other way in Los Angeles when it involved bootlegging and gambling in the early 1900s. They received such huge payoffs that ignorance of any crime was more profitable than was the conviction of criminals.

It was something of an embarrassment for the police when a rookie policeman stumbled onto the landing of bootleg liquor on the coast between Ventura and Santa Monica.

The police had been paid off, but the rookie cop who discovered the operation had not been informed.

Police just as casually ignored bookmaking, slot machines, and other gambling games. Police were more diligent in stopping "outside" gambling operators from coming into the city. They didn't want them infringing on the activity already there.

Potential interlopers were promptly put on a return train. The police knew where their bread was buttered, and they didn't want outsiders ruining it.

Even Al Capone knew he was in the wrong territory when he arrived in California in 1927. When asked by Los Angeles police what he was doing there, he assured them he was only vacationing. It was a great deal of relief for the local police when Capone boarded a train headed for Chicago.

From 1929 to 1933, Los Angeles was a wide-open city. Mayor John C. Porter had been a railway station attendant and then a used-car dealer before becoming mayor. Not only was he well aware of the criminal activity taking place in the city, but so were the police chief, the district attorney and the city attorney.

The city attorney and his wife were known to preside over the prostitution openly taking place within Los Angeles.

Driving gangsters and racketeers from Los Angeles became the big campaign cry of councilman Frank Shaw. He promised a government free from graft and corruption if voters would elect him to replace Mayor Porter.

Shaw was elected. One of his first acts, however, was to reinstate the police chief. He then put his brother, Joe Shaw, on his office staff. A vice squad of police officers were to operate out of the office under the brother.

Los Angeles reform groups soon found that it was Joe Shaw that was the go-between who had collected campaign money from the very racketeers Mayor Shaw had promised to oust.

Things were so corrupt in Los Angeles in 1931 that a group of prime movers founded the "Minute

Men", an offshoot of the Junior Chamber of Commerce. No one but the secretary of the organization knew the names of all its members.

The Minute Men conducted intensive investigations into the affairs of the city and county of Los Angeles. The group looked at purchases of material, searched past grand jury proceedings, and activities of county supervisors and city administrators.

Once the group felt it had sufficient evidence to show wrongdoing, it began to publish the information. The county supervisors and the district attorney reacted violently. Even the Los Angeles Times and the Examiner railed against the group. Only the Los Angeles Evening News offered support.

Known gunmen shadowed the Minute Men, and attempted to crash the group's secret meetings. A reporter for the Los Angeles Evening News was waylaid and beaten while investigating grand jury tampering.

The Minute Men then gave their findings to the state's legislature. Three Minute Men traveled to Sacramento to testify before a joint committee of the legislature.

Some politicians rose up in anger over the operations of the Minute Men, and publisher William Randolph Hearst ask the committee to withdraw its investigation as it was "not in the best interest of Los Angeles." The measure before the committee was tabled.

It wasn't until 1937, when a courageous new grand jury was empanelled that any real cure for corruption began to take place. Clifford E. Clinton, owner of Clifton's Cafeterias and the son of Salvation Army workers, headed this group.

Clinton operated his cafeterias on the basis of the Golden Rule. During the depression, he offered to feed anyone at his cafeterias that could not pay.

He was so intent on ridding the city of corrupt politicians that he organized Citizens Independent Vice Investigating Committee (CIVIC). The group was said to be composed of at least 500 outstanding business, church and public organizations. Clinton paid for grand jury and CIVIC investigations out of his own pocket.

When Clinton brought witnesses to testify before the grand jury, some were beaten or arrested and held incommunicado by the police. Clinton, himself, at one point, was cited for contempt by the grand jury. In October, 1937, the Clinton home on Los Feliz was bombed, blowing off the whole rear portion of the house.

Clinton was not to be intimidated. Harry Raymond, Clinton's chief investigator began turning up more and more of the truth on the criminal operations within the city.

Soon after, having been shadowed by police and had wire taps placed on his phone, Raymond stepped into his car only to be blown clear out of it by a blast of dynamite.

A neighbor dragged him to safety, where he lay half-dead. Raymond survived, and it spelled the beginning of the end for the Shaw gang in the mayor's office. The head of the vice squad and two of his officers operating out of the office were convicted of planting the explosive.

A recall election put reform party candidate Fletcher Bowron, a former judge, into office, and he began the real cleanup of Los Angeles. A number of criminal activities within the city were closed down and organized gamblers and racketeers left town.

Many of the gamblers and racketeers simply moved to Las Vegas, where they found the climate more receptive to their methods of operation.

Chapter 22

The Scotch Bar Case

'*All the legal talent in San Francisco was there*'

The scene at the little mining community of Scotch Bar was growing angry. At issue was which group of miners was entitled to the discovery of "rich gravel" recently found at the gold camp.

Two parties of prospectors were both laying claims to the find. As Charles Howard Shinn wrote in the San Francisco Bulletin, there were about a dozen men in each party, both seemingly honest in their belief that the gold rightfully belonged to them.

"It began to look more and more like fighting," Shinn reported.

Each group kept recruiting other miners to join their side, until finally there were twenty or thirty men ready to battle the same number on the other side.

As the rival groups took up their stations on the banks of the gulch, armed with bowie knives, revolvers, and shotguns, tempers began to rise. Eventually, eight or ten shots were fired, but no one was hurt.

The shots did attract dozens and even hundreds of men to the scene, however, who wanted to put down the hostilities long enough to negotiate a truce. Both parties agreed to settle the issue, but not by an ordinary trial.

They did not want a "miners'" court, or a "miners' committee" to make a ruling. They decided on what they believed to be a better plan.

The two groups chose a committee that would travel to San Francisco and engage three or four of the best lawyers they could find to represent each side. They also selected a judge with a great deal of experience in mining cases to arbitrate the issue.

"It was a great day at Scotch Bar," Shinn wrote, "when all this legal talent arrived to decide the ownership of the most valuable group of claims on the river. These claims had been lying absolutely idle once a truce plan was devised, untouched by any one, and guarded only by camp opinion and by the sacred pledges of honor ever since the day of the compact between the rival companies."

While not reported in any of the California law books, the Scotch Bar case took on all the formality that might have occurred had it been within the civil jurisdiction of a district court.

The lawyers and the judge were there to settle the case, Shinn says, adding that the entire camp wanted the case settled. More-so, both parties to the dispute were anxious to find out who the true owners would be.

To show the sense of fairness that prevailed in the mining camp, it should be noted that before the case began, both parties had agreed the winners of the case would pay all costs of the trial. It was felt the losers should not be made poorer still by being saddled with these expenses.

There would be no compromise as far as a verdict. There would be a clear winner and a clear loser.

"The defeated party took it placidly, without a murmur," Shinn writes. Nor was there ever heard a later complaint from the losers about how the decision went.

The winning party began mining the claim to a large audience of townspeople. The ravine on both sides of the claim was lined with men to observe the gold being taken out of the ground with "iron spoons", filling pans with solid gold. The mine was said to have been worth hundreds of thousands of dollars before the gold was finally exhausted.

The more valuable thing that came out of the Scotch Bar case, however, is the fact that the community, which arrived at such a sane way of deciding the issue, could be trusted to the utmost.

Such a community could be put down on a desert island and be trusted to organize a government, pick out its best men, punish its criminals, protect its higher interests, and develop local institutions.

The Siskiyou region where Scotch Bar was located did not monopolize that habit of self control. It existed in virtually every mining camp from Klamath to Colusa, and From Siskiyou to Fresno. Some were ruled better than others, but all were ruled well.

Chapter 23

The Lost Gunsight Mine

'*A man could lose 20 pounds in one day*'

The Indians called the place Tomesha, or "ground afire". The place is Death Valley, where the sun blazes down from May to October with the force of a blast furnace.

A man caught in such a place can drink as much as a gallon of water an hour and still not have enough. The body dehydrates at such a pace that travelers without water can lose 20 pounds in a single day---if he survives.

Caught in this inferno of a valley was a man named Martin, whose first name is lost in history. He was at the point of starvation when he spotted an elk moving among the rocks. Pulling out his rifle, he found the gunsight was missing.

In desperation, Martin grabbed a thin, wire-like piece of shale and wedged it into the slot where the gunsight should be. He took aim and killed the antelope.

It wasn't until young Martin reached Los Angeles, weeks later, that he took the rifle to a gunsmith for repairs. The gunsmith examined the piece of slate Martin had used as a rifle sight. It was pure silver.

The young man wanted nothing more to do with Death Valley, despite his rich discovery, and did not return. Yet, prospectors have searched for The Lost Gunsight ever since. It has become one of the legends of lost mines in the West.

Largest Gold Nugget

The largest single piece of gold found during the Gold Rush was located in Calaveras County in November, 1854, and weighed 161 pounds.

Even when twenty pounds is discounted for the amount of quartz the giant nugget contained, it was still worth $34,000 at prices at that time.

If a price of $150 per ounce is used to value the nugget, a value which later occurred, the large chunk of gold would have been valued at $338,400, and probably more as a collectors item or museum piece.

Not many miners actually found lumps of gold. Miners inevitably exaggerated the amounts they did find.

There are detractors, however, who claim the Lost Gunsight may be only myth.

Myth or not it didn't take long for the word of the silver "gunsight" to spread. Within the year, prospectors began their search, but found little for their trouble.

Ten years later, Dr. Darwin French organized an expedition whose aim was to find the Lost Gunsight

121

Mine. It too ended in failure. So did those of Dr. George, a member of French's party, who tried again a year later.

In 1873, another trio set out. It was W.T. Henderson's second trip into Death Valley looking for the silver lode. Traveling with Henderson were Robert Stewart and R.C. Jacobs.

While the group did not find The Lost Gunsight, they did come upon a ledge of silver in an area now known as "Surprise Canyon". The ore assayed out at four thousand dollars a ton.

The three men filed 80 location notices and thus began the establishment of Panamint City, which would become one of the real roaring camps of the West.

News of the discovery attracted the dregs of society to the new town. Thugs, gamblers, painted ladies, teamsters, prospectors, along with greenhorns, came running to this new silver country, bringing everything they had except money.

John Percival Jones and his partner, Senator Stewart of Virginia City, supplied the money. The pair organized the Panamint Mining Company. The first mill began processing the silver ore on April 29, 1875.

There was such a clamor to get in on the action in what was once a deserted spot in Death Valley, that Panamint City soon had forty saloons dishing out whiskey to the miners.

To open a saloon the only absolute requisites were a barrel or two of alcoholic compound and utensils for dishing it up to the customers.

The only safe in town was located at Harris and Rhine, a mercantile. The store's patrons deposited their mine payrolls in the safe. In one tale, a clerk arrived early at the store and was confronted by an armed pair he had thought were customers.

"Open the safe and count out the money," they ordered.

As the clerk's count reached four thousand dollars, one of the armed robbers, said, "This'll do for now. We'll come back and get the rest some other time---there are too many bandits around town."

Wells Fargo refused to open an office in Panamint. The firm considered the area so dangerous that it would be unable to protect its coaches with their shipments.

Some say it is the first time that Wells Fargo, who itself maintained a well-armed organization of detectives and armed guards, had declined to match wits and Winchesters.

Shipping the silver from Panamint became a problem. No one wanted to dig the silver ore and go to the expense of smelting it into bullion, only to have it hijacked as it was taken through the tortuous confines of Surprise Canyon.

Jones and Stewart outwitted any bandits by casting their silver inside seven hundred-pound cannon balls, taking them out of Panamint in open, unguarded wagons. No thefts were ever reported.

When Panamint City petered out, the search for The Lost Gunsight continued. The legend persists today, still luring prospectors to Death Valley.

(This ad was published in the Death Valley Chuck-Walla, April 1, 1907)

Chapter 24

California's Last 'Wild' Indian

'Ishi was a prehistoric man in a modern age'

The land where the Yahi tribe of California Indians existed was a region of endless ridges and cliff-walled canyons. When the last survivor of this small tribe was found, he wore little, if any clothing, despite the fact it was now forty years after the tribe had been considered extinct.

The Yahi tribe frequented the very wild area along Mill and Deer creeks, east of the Sacramento River in the very northern region of California.

Except during times when heavy snows and turbulent weather brought them to the verge of starvation, the Yahi moved about their small hillside community, safe from intrusion by the white man.

The Yahi was one of four dialectic divisions of the Yana tribe. It comprised only 300 to 400 souls at its utmost.

These Indians suffered heavily at the hands of white men, but were also subjected to frequent attacks by other Indian tribes. The Yahi were never even partially sheltered by reservations. They survived strictly by their wiles and their instincts.

The region where the Yahi lived contained patches in which the brush was almost impenetrable. There were many caves in the faces of the cliffs, providing the diminishing tribe with hundreds of places to hide from their real or supposed enemies.

The small tribe might not have survived as long as it did except for the fact the area had few minerals, no marketable lumber, and no rich bottom lands to attract the American newcomers.

The Yahi had settled into the region, giving them a retreat from which they could conveniently raid other regions, but at the same time provided them with a position virtually impenetrable by their enemies. Only a concerted plan by outsiders could ever rout them.

Enemy action inevitably came around 1865. It occurred after numerous skirmishes with small parties of Americans. In one disastrous fight, more often labeled as a slaughter, a large contingent of the Yahi Indians was surrounded and literally exterminated in an early-morning attack by a group of settlers.

For years the tribe was believed extinct. There were infrequent reports that a cattleman or a hunter had spotted "wild and naked Indians" who fled like deer. Other reports noted that deserted cabins in the hills had been rifled. Settlers in and around the Mill Creek area generally scoffed at these stories.

When the white invasion of California began, the Yahi escaped the fate of other Indian tribes, who tended to become hangers-on of the coming civilization. The Yahis followed their own time-honored rule and took refuge in their foothill retreats, remaining a so-called "wild" tribe.

But the white men settling the area refused to leave these Indians be. If a sheep was eaten by a mountain lion, it was blamed on the Indians. If provisions in a remote cattle camp turned up missing, it was sure to be the sneaky work of the Indians. Murders committed in out-of-the-way places were attributed to the Indians.

According to the "Handbook of Indians of California," the last printed reference to the Yahi is that of Stephen Powers, an anthropologist who knew them by their Maidu name of Kombo.

Powers told of how two men, two women, and a child, were encountered by a couple of hunters, but the Indians soon escaped into the brush. They were considered the last survivors of the Yahi group.

But in 1908, a party of surveyors working half way up the side of Deer Creek Canyon ran their line almost into a hidden camp in which four middle-aged and elderly Indians were living. The four fled to the brushy hillsides.

In the camp, surveyors found arrows, implements, baskets, stored food and some American objects, which obviously had been stolen.

What was more clear is that for 43 years, this tiny Indian household had remained unknown, a remnant of what was once a nation.

The remnant group had sustained itself by hiding in sheltered spots, smothering their camp smoke, and crawling under brush so as to leave no trail. Their ingenuity at eluding their white pursuers showed a marvelous instinct.

In 1911, a single survivor of the Yahi remained. He was alone, weaponless, and, pressed by hunger, was found approaching a slaughterhouse near

127

Oroville, where he was arrested and put into jail. His jailers, however, treated him kindly.

The fact that he was considered the last wild Indian in the United States drew wide interest. There was little question of the genuineness of his aboriginal condition. He was practically naked, in obvious terror, and knew no English.

His name was Ishi, an anglicized translation of which means man. Ishi was placed into the hands of T.T. Waterman, an anthropologist at the University of California, who had traveled to Oroville to pick up his charge.

The trip back to San Francisco entailed taking a train. As the train neared, Ishi only wanted to hide behind something. He had seen such trains before, but only in the distance, and did not realize they ran on tracks. He had always lain down in the grass or hid behind a bush or tree until the train monsters were out of sight.

Waterman notes in one article, printed in the book, "California Heritage", that Ishi was not so amazed by the tall buildings of San Francisco as he was by the crowds of people.

"He never ever became quite comfortable when a crowd gathered around," Waterman said, "even though he learned they meant no harm."

Ishi's failure to be impressed by the architecture of the city was credited to the possibility that, to Ishi, the tall buildings were not dissimilar to the cliffs and crags of his native mountains.

He was also more impressed with the trolley cars of San Francisco than with automobiles. It was the clang and noise of the trolleys that caught his attention, and especially the "whoosh" sound from the air brakes. He would watch the trolleys endlessly, attempting to figure out their workings.

Ishi did not like food that came with gravies and sauces. Neither did he like boiled foods. Give him fried, baked, roasted, broiled, or raw, and he was quite satisfied. He would not drink milk, nor touch eggs unless they were hard-boiled, claiming such foods led to colds in the head. Ishi wanted his food dry and clean appearing.

This last of the Yahi tribe learned to speak English slowly and brokenly, and would converse on all topics in his own tongue, with the exception of the fate of his kinsmen. On this subject, he was silent. Ishi never learned to shake hands.

Waterman, in his writings, noted, "I feel myself that in many ways he was perhaps the most remarkable personality of his century." Ishi's life ended in1916, when he was about 50 or 55 years old, due to a bout with tuberculosis to which he had never developed immunity.

Chapter 25

The Ice Harvest

'Fifteen miles of the Truckee River supplied ice throughout the West'

As California boomed, so did the need for ice. People in San Francisco and Sacramento were willing to pay high prices for this scarce commodity. This made ice harvesting big business in the Truckee area from 1868 through the 1920s.

The ice harvest, according to the Truckee-Donner Historical Society, in its publication, "Fire and Ice", was indeed one of the important factors in Truckee's development.

Customers wanted their drinks chilled, ice was needed to chill California's produce, and it was used to cool mine shafts in Nevada, where temperatures reached 140 degrees below ground.

San Francisco and Sacramento were both getting their ice from Boston in the early 1800s. The ice was brought by sailing ship. These ice shipments were expensive and undependable and customers welcomed a source closer at hand.

In 1853, the American-Russian Commercial Company entered the ice harvesting picture. This company later dominated the ice market. The company forced Boston suppliers out of the West Coast market. Boston could not compete with Sitka and Kodiak Alaska.

Ice Harvest began in Truckee in 1868. The harvest lasted from one to several weeks, depending on the size of a pond.
(From collection of Tom Maculay)

Ice became a competitive commodity. Horace Hale opened Summit Ice company at Lake Angela on Donner Summit; Joseph M. Graham and the Central Pacific established warehouses and ice ponds at Serene Lake, and Thomas McAuley and Robert Egbert opened Summit Valley Ice Company.

It was the Truckee River Basin that brought down the cost of ice, and the Summit companies and the Alaskan firm could not compete. Even the Summit firms were forced to relocate to the Truckee River Basin when the Central Pacific reached that area.

The Boca Mill and Ice Company used its pond for lumbering in the summer and for ice harvesting in the winter. By 1869, the firm had built an ice house with a capacity of eight-thousand tons. Still, other ice companies continued to crowd the area.

The fierce competition for a market that was limited led to serious attempts to control the ice market. Nevada Ice Company, Summit Ice Company, and Boca Mill and Ice Company, formed an umbrella over a company called Pacific Ice Company, although the three firms retained their individual identities and operation, allowing them to increase profits.

In 1875, Boca Brewing Company opened, becoming an immediate success, until it was destroyed by fire in 1893. The brewing company is said to have brought more fame to Boca than any of the ice companies ever did.

When experiments showed that ice could be used to cool produce shipments as they left California for the east coast, the Great Pacific Fruit Express was born. This created a new demand for ice. The People's Ice Company began operations at Bronco, and the Crystal Ice Company, and Mutual Ice Company, both opened near Verdi, Nevada.

Horses were used to scrape snow from the surface of ice ponds and expose the clear, hard ice. Tony Ghirard, a Truckee blacksmith who died in 1981, told of making ice shoes for the horses so they wouldn't slip while hauling huge blocks of ice.

Once the ice surface was exposed, it was scribed into a giant checkerboard. A common block size, according to historian Tom Macaulay, of Reno, was 22 inches square, but some companies preferred 22 inches by 32 inches.

Ice was usually cut at two-thirds its depth, explains Macaulay. For ice blocks twelve inches deep, this meant making a cut of eight inches, leaving a lip on the bottom of four inches which was necessary to support the weight of the men and horses in the harvest crew.

Ice blocks are moved along the channel where ice has been removed and sent to ice house by conveyor.
(From Tom Maculay Collection)

As the first blocks were removed, it opened a long float channel. Long lines of men would then guide rafts of ice along the float channel to an elevator where steam engines would lift it to storage houses.

Harvesters removed and stored as much as sixty tons of ice per hour. In some years, the Truckee ice harvests stored 300,000 tons of ice.

Bad weather was the greatest detriment to ice harvest. Rain would soften the ice, sometimes destroying the ice crop.

Snow was just as bad. It could submerge the ice sheet, and allow pond water to flow in, covering the existing ice sheet, and likewise ruin the ice crop.

While ice was harvested in Truckee, the market was controlled in San Francisco. Owners of ice companies met in San Francisco in 1882, resulting in the formation of still another new company, Union Ice Company.

Six different companies pooled their resources to form "the Union", five of which was harvesting ice in the Sierra. At the time of its formation, Union Ice was a distributing company, but soon began to acquire its own harvesting and manufacturing facilities.

In 1884, two other companies, Truckee Ice Company at Martis Creek, and Crystal Ice Company, of San Francisco, came in to challenge the dominating Union Ice. Tahoe Ice Company also entered the fray, becoming one of the largest and most successful independent companies.

Three strong companies now vied for the ice trade. Union Ice and National Ice companies had the strongest financial backing. Tahoe Ice was small but efficient.

Over the next nine years, these three companies engaged in bitter competition, with the smaller Tahoe Ice playing the two giants against each other. National Ice eventually gained a controlling interest in the stock of Tahoe Ice Company, leaving only two ice firms.

From 1868 until 1927, the Truckee Basin supplied ice for the western markets. It was this ready supply of ice that made the formation of Pacific Fruit Express possible.

Competition from artificial ice forced the gradual closing of the ice ponds in the Truckee Basin. By 1919, all of the ice harvesting sites were owned by The Union Ice Company.

There were twenty six or more companies operating on the Truckee before the business died. There is little today to mark the sites of the historic ice harvests. The storage warehouses were demolished or destroyed by fire.

Chapter 26

The Mormons

'Every girl needs a husband, even if she has a head three-feet long.'

San Bernardino was established as a Mormon colony. It was expected early on to become a second Salt Lake City.

The Mormons held strong views and defended them, especially on the subject of polygamy. The women, as well as the men, were apparently happy in polygamy.

Orson Pratt's statement, in an attempt to explain the Mormon philosophy, said, "A man can love more than one wife in the same manner that he can love more than one child. What faithful, virtuous woman would prefer to stand as the sixth or seventh wife of a good and faithful man rather than to have no husband at all."

Heber Kimball, another faithful Mormon, had even stronger views. "Every girl should have a husband, even if she has a head three feet long."

Brigham Young himself married eight times in one year and had thirty wives and fifty-six children.

One wife expressed the belief that Mormon women had easier access to Heaven than others, and that any suffering here below only added laurels to the crown above.

Nancy Ashton, one of 12 spouses maintained by her Mormon husband, dealt with her situation in another way. Her husband would place a card on the door of the wife he intended to visit that particular night. Nancy delighted in switching the cards around.

Another Mormon wife, Prudence Gamble, may have summed up best the feeling of how the wives felt to be one of several chosen by a husband. "I would rather have a third interest in a first-rate man, than a first interest in a third-rate man."

The southern part of California remained a thinly populated, often lawless, cattle frontier. The arrival of the Mormons in San Bernardino established that area as a Mormon colony, and an outpost of Brigham Young's Salt Lake City empire.

Without delay, on their arrival in 1851, the Mormons set about developing farms, building irrigation works, and laying out a city.

Elders Amasa M. Lyman and Charles C. Rich commanded the train of 150 wagons that brought the Mormon colonists to San Bernardino.

In their letters, they note the site was selected "in view of forwarding the gathering of the Saints from abroad, and from Europe in particular, by this route, should we be enabled to settle in this country as we wish."

It is noteworthy that Brigham Young did not like the idea of such a large contingent of his Saints moving to southern California. He refused to endorse or bless their journey. The southern California Mormon settlers still deferred to the advice of their

137

Salt Lake City leader once they became settled, however.

A threat by Indian chief Antonio Garra to massacre every white man in southern California caused a major change in the plans of the San Bernardino Mormons.

Instead of individual homes, they built a fort from which they could better protect themselves. Even though the Garra revolt was soon extinguished, the Mormons continued living in the fort for more than a year.

In 1853, only two years after their arrival, the industrious Mormons had their valley humming. There were grapes coming off the vines planted by Bishop Tenny. Fruit trees were thriving, and a better road had been built linking San Bernardino to Los Angeles, as well as a new route to San Diego that would carry any surplus foods and products the Mormons could produce.

There was a flour mill to process the wheat grown on some 4,000 acres of Mormon land. Several sawmills, operated by the swift mountain streams, were turning out lumber for houses and for the stores the Saints were now building.

The Mormons believed the property they purchased in 1851 comprised 80,000 to 100,000 acres. The U.S. Land Commission gave the Mormons the dismal word that their purchase contained only eight square leagues of land, less than half what they thought they were buying.

During their settlement period, the Mormons had to contend with a number of squatters. At Yucaipa lived John Brown, an Independent, as those who were not Mormons were called. He began raising cattle on land the Mormons claimed to own. When ordered to vacate within ten days, he refused, and at the same time, stirred up others in the community with grievances against the church, including some ex-Mormons, who sided with Brown.

The squatter eventually withdrew from Yucaipa, but the Mormons were soon faced with problems from another front. This uproar involved Bishop Tenney, who was sent out to preach among the rancherias. The Indians, at the time, outnumbered the whites.

When the bishop returned, accusations were floated that he was negotiating with the Indians to join the Mormons in driving out those who opposed them.

Bishop Tenney denied the charge, explaining his mission had been to ask the Indians to believe in the Lord Jesus Christ, to leave off all drunkenness, thievery, and gambling, and to live in peace with their white neighbors. Resentment against the Mormons continued, nonetheless.

San Bernardino remained a distinctly Mormon community until 1858 when the Mountain Meadows Massacre and a threatened conflict with the federal government led Brigham Young to recall the colonists to Salt Lake City.

At the time of the withdrawal, there were about 100 improved farms in the settlement, besides the flour mills, the sawmills, stores, and irrigation projects. Most of this was sold to gentile settlers at a small fraction of the actual value.

Chapter 27

The Rocking Stone

'This 17-ton stone could be rocked by a human hand'

A short distance from the Truckee railroad station, is a curious creation of nature. It is called the "Rocking Stone" by the people in the area.

While noted naturalist John Muir's inspection of this freak of nature was that it was formed by glacial action, the Indians in the area told a different tale.

The thing that made this stone formation unique was the fact that sitting atop a flat-topped granite stone rising some 30-feet high and as many feet in diameter, was another stone.

This second stone measured some six feet in both height and diameter, and was tapered at the base. The top rock was perched so delicately on the wide, bottom stone, that it could be rocked back and forth with the push of a human hand, even though it weighed several tons.

According to the version of the Indians, long before the coming of the white man, members of the Washoe tribe pitched their wigwams around the great granite formation. At that time there was only the wide, base stone.

Since prowling animals could not climb the sides of the stone, Indians would place their meat upon its flat shelf-like top, drying the food for winter use.

This is a 1901 photo of the rocking stone.
(Courtesy of Truckee Donner Historical Society)

But one day, while the men were out hunting and fishing, and the Indian women and children tended the campfires, a great flock of birds descended upon the stone and carried away all of the meat.

This happened time and again, and the Indians were looking at scant food supplies for the winter. The Washoes decided drastic measures were needed. They prayed to their gods for help. The Wind God, the Indian's say, took pity on them and caused a great storm that darkened the sun.

When the storm stopped, the Indians gave a cry of thanksgiving. There, on top of the massive, mesa-like boulder was perched another stone, "as like the great rock as a youth is like his father."

Now, when the birds came to steal the Indian's drying meat, the Wind God would breathe upon the stone, rocking it to and fro, much like a treetop in the wind, frightening the birds away.

Legend says that as long as the Washoes lived in the area, there was always an abundance of dried fish and meat to carry them through the harsh winters.

C.F. McGlashan, editor of The Truckee Republican, later purchased the hillside where the Rocking Stone still sits.

Around the stone itself, McGlashan built a 14-sided tower. The odd structure was used as a private museum for the rusted utensils, wagon irons, and other relics he had excavated from the Donner Party cabin sites, along with a collection of butterflies and moths that he maintained.

On top of a flagpole located on the roof of the tower structure, McGlashan placed an electric arc light, which he turned on every night, giving the hillside an eerie glow.

Mrs. George Hinkle, a daughter of McGlashan, noted, "Not infrequently wild-eyed train passengers, wakened from a deep sleep to catch a glimpse of the glowing, wraith-like edifice, and would wonder querulously what in God's name that thing was up on the hill."

There are reportedly 24 such stone formations as the Rocking Stone in various parts of the world.

Unfortunately, the Rocking Stone no longer rocks. It has not rocked in years and today may be more a symbol of Truckee's past than a true curiosity.

The Rocking Stone as it looks today in its enclosure.

It was deemed necessary to shore up the stone to protect it from vandalism or other accidents, such as crashing down the hillside into the center of town.

There was fear the 17-ton Rocking Stone could roll off its granite pedestal and do great harm.

Chapter 28

Turning Indians into Cowboys

'Their love of horsemeat made the padres wary'

It is considered fortunate for the Spaniards then building the California missions that Indians did not have horses.

Early California law decreed that no Indians should be allowed to own or ride a horse. It was feared that unfriendly mounted Indians could mean serious trouble, a fear that was justified later during the late 18th Century.

It is doubtful whether California Indians at the time had ever seen a horse before the Spaniards arrived.

The first cattle were introduced to Santa Barbara County in 1782. At that time, the area defined as Santa Barbara County in 1850 included present-day Ventura County. This comprised an area as large as the State of Connecticut.

Spanish friars and leather-jacketed soldiers representing King Carlos drove stringy longhorn cattle from Mexico to provide beef for the garrison of the Royal Presidio at Santa Barbara.

These early Spanish cattle brought to the missions were quite tame and easy to corral. But as the cattle

145

population increased, some missions were forced to turn their cattle loose on open rangelands to forage for sufficient grass.

As time went on, there were not enough Spanish vaqueros to handle the increasing cattle herds. Gradually, the cattle population outgrew the mission properties and became wild.

The market for hides and tallow boomed and the demand for work hands to do these tasks grew with it. The cattle needed to be rounded up. The need for cowboys was so great, Spanish authorities soon turned a deaf ear to the law forbidding Indians to ride horses.

The mission padres decided to selected the most promising young Indians to train as vaqueros. Each Indian was given a blanket, a "taparrabo" (breechcloth) and a twilled blouse.

In his book, "Cowboy Culture," David Dary described some of the problems faced with the cowboy proteges. "While the padres taught the Spanish language to the new recruits, often they had to learn the Indians' language first."

In selecting the Indian vaquero, the padres generally looked for those with strength and endurance. At the same time, they needed Indians who could be trusted, as the cattle gathering work would take them miles from the mission and away from the watchful eyes of the padres.

More-so, the padres needed Indians who could not only be trusted with the cattle, but of greater importance, with the horses. By the time the padres began to train converts as vaqueros in California, the Indians had developed a fondness for beefsteak and a greater love of horsemeat. To them the steak of a horse was a delicacy.

146

The problem for the padres was to make sure the Indians selected as cowboys would keep the horses they rode underneath them and not end up in a rangeland barbecue.

Once the Indians were tested and selected, they were taught the art of roping, how to hobble, throw, and saddle a horse, and how to use a hackamore. The word "hackamore" is a corruption of the Spanish word "jaquima", meaning halter.

The fears that mounted Indians would mean trouble did come to pass. During the 1850s and 1860s, Indians from San Joaquin and Owens River valleys carried off hundreds of horses and cattle from the ranchos of Los Angeles and Santa Barbara counties. San Diego and San Luis Obispo suffered almost as severely from the depredation of Indians from other districts.

One newspaper editor estimated that San Fernando Mission alone lost nearly a thousand horses annually, and that in five years, Indian horse thieves had cost the rancheros of the southern counties at least three hundred thousand dollars.

The secularization of the missions, beginning in the early 1830s, spelled the end of the long-established guardianship of the padres over cattle range being held in trust for the Indians. California governors began granting vast areas of land to the new ruling class, the rancheros.

Chapter 29

Justice in San Francisco

'They learned how to cope with street gangs'

Youthful street gangs pervaded San Francisco in 1849, brought on in part by the sudden influx of gold into the city, and by a brash desire to defy society's norms.

There were the "Hounds," sometimes called the "Regulators". From another particulary notorious part of the city, Sydney Town, were the "Sydney Ducks".

These gangs were generally made up of adventurous social parasites, criminals, and other elements determined to assert the own rights above others, at whatever cost.

The Sydney Ducks was composed of former members of Great Britain's prison colony in Australia. San Francisco residents would comment, "The Sydney Ducks are cackling" after one of the gang's troubling forays.

One Sunday, July 15, 1849, San Franciscans became particularly incensed when a large and rowdy crowd from the Regulators held what was termed a "patriotic" parade. These scoundrels toured various saloons, demanding liquor and smashing windows as they reeled down the streets. Soon, they began to brutally assault some Chilean families living in tents on the city's sand dunes.

Hangings were used as a deterrent to San Francisco's street gangs. Justice was just as stern in the mining camps.
(California State Library)

As they beat, kicked, and fired upon the Chileans, city elders decided they had had enough. Sam Brannan, one of the city fathers, gathered other elders and property owners around him and formed citizens' court.

The court found the leader of the Regulators guilty, and banned him and a score of his cohorts from the city.

149

This did not stop the violence and criminality of the San Francisco gangs. Murderers and thieves went unpunished, and there was no sign that city government officials would or could act against them. The need for law and order stirred the citizens to act again.

"The Committee of Vigilance of San Francisco" was formed on June 10, 1850, comprised of some 200 members.

The members determined in their stated policy, "no thief, burglar, incendiary, or assassin, shall escape punishment, either by the quibbles of the law, the insecurity of prisons, the carelessness or corruption of the police, or a laxity of those who pretend to administer justice."

Scarcely had the organization taken shape when its members were summoned to meet by two sharp peals from the city's fire bell.

The committee was called to contend with one John Jenkins, a former convict from Sydney, Australia. Jenkins had burglarized a shipping office on Commercial Street, defying anyone to stop him as he carried away the strongbox.

When Vigilantes members tried to stop him, he brazenly tossed the strongbox into San Francisco Bay in an act of further contempt.

In a hasty trial, Jenkins was pronounced guilty. He was taken to Portsmouth Square where Vigilantes hastily erected a gallows. Jenkins was hanged on the spot.

A coroner's jury claimed that Sam Brannon, who had acted as judge, and others on the Vigilante jury, were hasty and harsh in their treatment of the

Australian. San Francisco's "best citizens", however, applauded the action.

The Vigilante committee was called to action again by the firehouse bell on July 11, 1851. This case involved another member of the Sydney Ducks, one "English Jim" Stuart, a confessed criminal.

The committee, through a case of mistaken identify, had very nearly convicted the wrong man for Stuart's crime. The law enforcement body quickly covered its mistake by finding Stuart guilty. Stuart was led to the Market Street Wharf and hanged from the yardarm of a ship anchored there.

The Vigilantes continued imposing their brand of justice on gang terrorists despite the actions of their legally appointed sheriff. Two men, Samuel Whittaker and Robert McKenzie were brought to trial and confessed their crimes. The Vigilantes condemned the men to die.

The sheriff stepped in, seized the prisoners, and put them in jail. The disgruntled Vigilantes re-abducted the two men and took them to their headquarters. As the firehouse bell announced the execution of Whittaker and McKenzie, six thousand people watched.

Records indicate during the two year tenure of the San Francisco Vigilantes, the following sentences were imposed on lawbreakers: 4 hanged; one man whipped; 14 men deported; one ordered to leave the state; handed over to authorities, 15. Forty-one others were discharged by the committee.

The final entry recorded in the Vigilante secretary's book was dated June 30, 1852.

Vigilante activity soon extended to the mining camps, where the self appointed lawmen were especially heavy-handed in imposing sentences against foreigners. In Downieville, a mining town on the Yuba River, a group of American Independence Day celebrants decided to impose their authority on Juanita, considered an "evil" Mexican woman.

Juanita fought back, killing one of the Vigilantes with a knife. She was hastily found guilty and sentenced to hang, even though some miners on the jury were repelled by the idea of hanging a woman. Juanita was "strung up" from a wooden bridge spanning the Yuba River.

Unfortunately, presumption of guilt too often was equivalent to conviction. At Marysville, 17 murders had occurred in one week. There were so many robberies occurring with such alarming frequency around Mokelumne Hill, that a Vigilante committee there felt compelled to act.

In its haste, the committee executed a scapegoat before nearly one thousand witnesses to satisfy the populace there. In addition to execution, punishment meted out to the miscreants included ear cropping and whipping.

Fiddletown Justice

Justice in Fiddletown and other mining communities was not always just. If evidence was lacking, it was often created. At other times, justice could be comical.

Big Annie was the hefty madam of a fandango parlor in the gold town of Columbia. As she lurched from a saloon one day, she came face to face with the town's highly respected school mistress, and forced the school teacher off the sidewalk.

When the schoolmistress simply lifted her skirts to hold them above the dust, Big Annie slapped her own plump thigh and shouted, "Who'd 'a thought it! The angel walks on two legs just like Annie."

This didn't sit well with the boys of Fire Engine Company No. 2. They decided Big Annie should not get away with her insults to the town's school teacher.

The firemen dropped their engine hoses into the State Street cistern and furiously manned their hand pumps, training a stream of water into Big Annie's parlor. The powerful stream washed the drunken Annie right out of her bed and into the middle of the street.

A more sober case involved the robbery of $9,000 from the Wells Fargo office. Five men were arrested, not because of any evidence, but because the men simply had bad reputations.

The lynch mob was determined it would produce evidence one way or another. The mob decided to string up the prisoners until they confessed. When the sheriff arrived from Jackson, there were no prisoners.

Fiddletown was supposedly named for the many Missouri fiddlers who came to the area. They took turns playing tunes while their partners mined the stream. One 1850, visitor, however, claimed there was not a fiddler to be found in Fiddletown.

There was one period when Fiddletown residents, tired of being the joke of its picturesque name. The town's fathers decided to change the name to "Oleta" which they considered more refined. It wasn't until a half-century later that signs at the entrance of town were changed back to Fiddletown.

Fiddletown also produced its own classic courtroom procedures. When a witness exhausted the court's patience with an outlandish story, the judge took care of the situation.

"I declare court adjoined," he would roar, and would then say, off the record, "This man is a damned liar." He quickly followed his opinion of the witness by immediately announcing, "Court is back in session."

In the mining town of Columbia, more than once mobs hauled a suspected criminal hell-bent down Broadway, carrying a rope with which to hang him from the high Gold Spring flume. One such incident was the hanging of John Barclay.

The occurrence involved a miner who accidentally broke a beer pitcher in Martha's Saloon. Martha, Barclay's wife, turned on the miner in a fury. The miner merely laughed, and shoved Martha into a chair.

Barclay himself then came storming through the saloon's swinging doors with six-shooters blazing, killing the miner. Barclay was arrested and jailed.

A mob scene developed, and a crowd of residents swinging axes, crowbars and other heavy weapons, smashed their way into the jail, bent on lynching Barclay.

A kangaroo court lasted less than five minutes, and Barclay was convicted and sentenced to death. When the Sheriff attempted to rescue the prisoner, he was clubbed with a pistol butt and dragged away.

Men from the mob scaled the flume's trestle, dangling the rope from its highest point. Men on the ground made the rope fast around Barclay's neck, and then began pulling him 40 feet above the heads of the milling crowd.

But the hangmen had neglected to tie the arms of Barclay, allowing him to grasp the rope above his head and hang on to keep from strangling. The men on the flume kept jiggling at the rope to shake Barclay loose, crying, "Let go, you damned fool! Let go!"

Barclay's grip finally weakened and his arms dropped to his sides, his body hanging limp at the rope's end. The mob then streamed back to Martha's Saloon and stoned all its windows. Shortly after midnight, the revelers reeled down the dark alleys of the town, and all was quiet in Columbia.

The only movement was Barclay's body drifting in the breeze as it dangled from the Gold Spring flume.

Chapter 30

Newport

'A harbor built by a river'

The saltwater playground of Newport went through a series of name changes before getting its current one.

It was first called "Bolsa Quigara" or "Bay of High Banks". Early maps later designated it as Bolsa de San Joaquin. The tideland areas were often called Cienega de las Ranas, or "Swamp of the Frogs."

The area was later referred to as "Gospel Swamp", due to the arrival of Isaac Hickley, an ex-Baptist preacher. The Reverend Hickley would hold services whenever an opportunity arose.

Newport's formation began in 1825, when the silt from the flooding Santa Ana River swept into the ocean. The ocean current gradually deposited the silt along the shore, builting up a peninsula.

Each new flood added more silt to the shoreline until it had extended almost to the bluffs on the Corona del Mar shore forming a nice harbor for small vessels.

In the winter, when the river rose to high levels, boats were necessary to reach the mainland to market produce from the district and to bring in supplies.

Two brothers, James and Robert McFadden, purchased a 1,000 acre section of swamp land around what is now Newport from the state for one dollar an acre. This gave the brothers control of the ocean frontage that is now Newport Beach. Their holdings included Balboa Island.

Workers employed by the McFadden brothers had difficulty mouthing the Spanish pronunciation of Bolsa de San Joaquin and of Cienega de las Ranas. They simply called the area Newport.

As farming expanded in the area, so did erosion, which eventually made the harbor unnavigable. James McFadden decided a pier should be built to accommodate the vessels that had to anchor in the open roadstead while their cargos were loaded on barges and poled to shore.

The pier was finished in 1888, and railroad tracks were laid on the pier to carry back cargo. Newport soon became an important lumber port.

The ever enterprising James McFadden next decided that a railroad should be built from Newport to Santa Ana. Not knowing what supplies he would need, he decided to measure the distance of the planned railroad, using a unique measuring device.

He tied a rag on the wheel of his buggy. As a railroad engineer drove the buggy, McFadden would count the revolutions as the wheel turned.

The first train ran in 1892, and the following year, the Newport Hotel was built, signaling that the area would become a vacation resort.

Both Newport and the tiny Balboa island kept developing. A settlement of summer vacationers originated on the island. Each family maintained a small sailing skiff to reach the mainland.

Soon, spirited boat races were held on the bay on Sundays, and Balboa became a yachtsman's paradise. There was still no yacht club for boaters as late as 1911. Those wanting to join such a group would affiliate with the South Coast Yacht Club at Los Angeles Harbor. Increased interest prompted the South Coast Yacht Club to open a branch in Newport Bay.

Other clubs formed as the vacation crowd grew. The Newport Harbor Yacht Club was formed in 1917, the Balboa Yacht Club formed in 1922 to promote small boat races, and the Lido Island Yacht Club came along in 1928.

Ferry service started connecting the tiny island to the peninsula in 1907.

Chapter 31

The Massacre at San Miguel

Bragging led to a dreadful and bloody slaughter

It was as if madmen had run through the mission, killing and ransacking everything in sight. It is a wretched and gruesome tale but definitely a part of San Miguel's history.

Mission San Miguel never ranked with the best of the missions. The land, though lying in the fertile bottom of the upper Salinas Valley, was difficult for the missionaries to cultivate. Hard frosts in the winter and scorching summer heat made farming near impossible.

The year was 1849, and the priests had already left their posts at Mission San Miguel because of secularization. What life had gone on at the mission under the padres had ceased. The adobe structure was now the home of Guillermo Reed, who grazed his sheep and cattle on what once were mission lands.

The mines in the gold country were making men rich, sometimes overnight, and Guillermo felt he could achieve wealth in the mines faster and more quickly than from his sheep and cattle raising.

One day, he said to his partner, Don Petronelo Rios, who was older than Reed, "Why don't we go to the mines, and get our share of what is going on there?

159

Mission San Miguel is mainly a tourist stop today, although services are held there.

All our acquaintances are getting rich, while we are muddling along here."

The pair did moderately well at the placers, but by no means to the extent that Reed had hoped. Unfortunately, the foolish young Reed was given to braggadocio, implying to those around him that they had indeed struck it rich.

The older and more sensible Don Petronelo did not like him talking so loose. "Here we are," Rios would say, "among all kinds of wild fellows, and it is not wise to make all this talk of the money we are supposed to have. We are in danger of losing the little we have made."

Tiring of the mines, Reed returned to his sheep and cattle at San Miguel, while Don Petronelo settled in Templeton. Reed was to oversee both his and his partner's livestock, which grazed at the mission. The mission was quiet and lonely, save for the presence of Reed and his family.

The granddaughter of Don Petronelo tells the grisly details of what happened that night.

"One evening a party of men came to the mission. There were three Americans, an Irishman, and an Indian who acted as a guide. The white men had known Mr. Reed at the mines, and he welcomed them accordingly. Still he kept up the pretence of having made lots of money at the mines."

When asked how much they had made, Reed laughed, "Oh, bags and bags of it! Why, that boy can hardly lift the smallest sack," he said, indicating his wife's little brother.

The miners lingered at San Miguel for several days. When they did prepare to leave, they purchased supplies, paying with twenty-dollar gold pieces.

Reed called the young boy to bring one of the "little" sacks of gold dust (the only one he had) so he could weigh out their change. Again, the men talked late into the night, and Reed invited them to stay over until morning.

As the fire burned low, one man went to get more wood. He returned, carrying an armload of wood, inside of which he concealed an axe. From behind, he struck Reed in the head, killing him instantly.

In the next room, Mrs. Reed, her three-year-old child and a nurse, were preparing for bed. The decadent miners rushed in, leaving them dead as well, along with a child in another room, who was bludgeoned as he slept. By the time they finished, nine people lay dead, including a lowly sheepherder.

After ransacking the building in search of the gold, the marauders dragged the bodies to the farthest room in the mission, where they threw them in a heap.

It was two days before the massacre was discovered. The sheriff in San Luis Obispo was notified. He ordered his deputies, "Don't attempt to take any prisoners. Shoot immediately."

The murderers were found near Gaviota. The Indian guide had deserted the foursome, who had treated him badly, making him kneel to eat instead of allowing him to sit at the table. The Indian feared he would be the next victim to die at their hands.

Two of the murderers were shot on the spot. The leader ran into the sea, throwing from his pockets the gold he had taken from the Reeds at the mission. He drowned while the officers fired at him.

The sole survivor was the Irishman, who surrendered and begged to be allowed to confess. Once he had done so, he, too, was shot.

It was years later, related Don Petronelo's granddaughter, when the Indian, who had been a guide to the four ruffians, was seen among the workers at her grandfather's ranch. When questioned about the events, he always acted as if he were "loco", and could never be induced to talk about the events that took place at the mission on that dreadful night.

Chapter 32

The Mojave Trail Slave Trade

'Women and children were commonly bartered'

The Mojave Desert was an important link in the slave trading of the southwest.

The ancient Mojave Indian Trail, a route stretching beyond the confines of the Mojave Desert itself, went from east of the Colorado River to the Mojave River and on across the San Bernardino Mountains to the Pacific Ocean.

Fray Francisco Hermenegildo Garces, in 1776, recorded incidents of slavery while he traveled the Mojave Indian Trail. Near Needles, where he encountered a group of Mojave Indians, Father Garces purchased two captive women slaves. He later released the women and sent them back to their own villages.

In another incident, Garces found Mojaves holding two captive Jalchedun women. The Jalchedun was one of the weaker of the Colorado River tribes. These women, too, Garces purchased after heated bargaining, paying the Mojaves "a poor horse and some other small presents." These two slaves were sent, with an old interpreter, back to their home with the Jalchedun tribe.

The origin of slavery among the Mojave Indians was undoubtedly connected with their warlike operations. The practice evolved from simply killing their enemies to that of using those captured for work and trade.

During a long prehistoric period, the Mojaves had captured or traded for women and children whom they took back to their villages along the Colorado River. Slave women were sometimes adopted, tattooed at puberty, and even married.

Olive Oatman was a white slave whom the Mojave purchased from the Apache. For five years she lived with the Mojave, during which she was tattooed. She later related the tribe's custom of killing a slave as a sacrifice should any member of the tribe be killed in battle.

A diary, kept by W.B. Lorton on his trip to California in 1849, graphically describes the extent to which selling of Indians took place. He wrote of meeting the Ute Indian Chief Walkara, the "Hawk of the Mountains", who was reputed to be a famous horse stealer and terror of the "Spanard (sic) and Piede."

The Piede Indians, were deep in poverty, said Lorton. "They increased too fast, and they sold their children for a 'plug of tobacco' for bondage in the Spanish ranchos."

In one instance, Lorton said Indians came into camp with an infant captive that they wanted to trade for a mule. The Americans talked the Indians into cleaning the child's face, but declined the purchase.

Walkara was acknowledged as the undisputed Mexican-Indian trafficker in human flesh. This cunning Ute chief, who fifteen years later was baptized into the Mormon faith, took captive women and children from the weak bands of Shoshonean stock in southern Utah, Nevada, and probably from the Mojave Desert, and sold them around Los Angeles.

The price of slaves in the markets of New Mexico varied with the age and quality of the person. Those from ten to fifteen years old sold from $50 to $100. Another historian, Warren Beck, said the price for a healthy Indian on the Santa Fe Market was $300.

Another writer, Gwinn H. Heap, who accompanied California Indian Agent E. E. Beale, said that annual expeditions were sent out of New Mexico to trade with Pah-Utahs for children.

Chapter 33

The Trip to Monterey

'They named the area as they traveled'

It was more than 150 years after Sebastian
Vizcaino had discovered Monterey Bay that Spain
attempted to cement control of the region. There were
rumblings of interest from other countries who might
want the area.

Spain's King Charles sent Jose de Galvez to
Mexico City as his special representative, or visitor-
general. Galvez was variously described as energetic,
efficient, and far-sighted on one hand, and mean,
jealous, crafty, supersitious and ridiculously vain on
the other.

From his Mexican seat of power, Galvez
dispatched two vessels to transport soldiers and
supplies to the port of Monterey. At the same time, an
overland expedition was dispatched from the Spanish
missions of Lower California, aiming for the same
destination.

In charge of this overland expedition was Don
Gaspar de Portola, and Fray Junipero Serra, Father
President of the Missions. A few days after reaching
San Diego, Portola recognized the San Diego port as a
royal presidio.

Historians have described the area as being in a forlorn and sorry state, with only a few brush huts in the depths of the wilderness in which resided a handful of scurvy-ridden men, surrounded by none too friendly Indians.

Gaspar de Portola thought he had miss calculated the location of Monterey Bay

When the Spaniards resumed their march northward under Portola's leadership, Father Serra stayed at San Diego to consecrate the first of the California missions and to minister to the sick who were unable to take the long trail to Monterey.

Spain's King Charles III, a vigorous and able statesman, ordered Don Gaspar de Portola to lead an expedition to develop an overland trail from San Diego in search of Vizcaino's Monterey. He was accompanied by Father Francisco Gomez and Father Juan Crespi, who kept a descriptive journal of the trip.

As Portola and his companions marched across the fertile plains and valleys near the coast, they made careful notes of the most desirable locations for settlements and missions. Every place of importance was given a name.

Ten days out of San Diego, the party felt a series of severe earthquakes, resulting in Father Crespi calling one stream, "the River of the Sweet Name of Jesus of the Earthquakes". The leather-jacketed soldiers on the mission simply called the river the Santa Ana.

The expedition traveled through an Indian village whose inhabitants were skillful at carving wooden canoes. The explorers named the place Carpinteria. Later, a soldier is said to have killed a sea gull where the trail turned from the coast inland to the Santa Inez Valley. They named that pass Gaviota.

The Spaniards saw populations of friendly Indians as they traveled through the country. The Indians were divided into many small tribes or clans, each living in its own village and speaking its own dialect.

Unlike other American Indians who knew at least the rudiments of agriculture, growing such things as corn, beans, and melons, the California Indians raised no crops of any kind.

Their diet was diverse. "They ate acorn meal, grass seeds, shell fish, small game, grasshoppers, insects, snakes, or anything else that ran, walked, crept, crawled or wriggled. They were great thieves, wore little or no clothing, and loved music and dancing," said historian Robert Glass Cleland.

From San Diego to the foot of the Santa Lucia Mountains, just beyond San Luis Obispo, the Portola expedition found an easy trail.

When the last of the company crossed the mountains, they followed along the Salinas River, which wound to the sea. Excitement peaked as they saw a point of land forested with many pines and a bay. The expedition was sure it had found the long lost port of Monterey discovered by Vizcaino.

The more the explorers examined the bay, however, the less it resembled the descriptions left by Vizcaino and Father Ascension, who had accompanied him.

They decided they would have to renew their search for Monterey. With supplies dangerously low, they trudged onward, coming to the present site of Watsonville, Point Reyes, and the Farallones. Examining their charts, they now realized they had overshot the port of Monterey.

Portola ordered the expedition to give up the search and return to San Diego. The half-starved men were forced to eat some of their worn-out pack animals on the return trip to keep alive.

After a brief rest, and loaded with new supplies, they set out again in search of Monterey. They reached the Salinas Valley without serious incident. On careful examination, they soon convinced themselves their first sighting truly had been the bay of Monterey behind the point of pines.

Portola quickly took steps to occupy the harbor which came to be known as "The Spanish Heart of California".

Portola is recognized by historians as the first Governor of Alta California. In 1775, the King of Spain named Monterey the Capital of California.

Chapter 34

The Stockton Gang Plow

'It changed farming in California and the West'

It was a wheat grower near Manteca in the San Joaquin Valley that changed farming throughout the world.

In 1860, Westley Underwood borrowed two plows belonging to his neighbors and connected them to his own. Each of the three plows had a ten-inch share. This was the first "three-bottom plow".

While the plow was indeed a time saver, it was still cumbersome. The three heavy timbers bolted diagonally across the beams made it awkward to handle. Worse, yet, the plow had no wheels.

Another wheat grower, Lowell Alexander, improved on the plow by placing the standards of the three plows on a single beam. He sold the patent rights to H.C. Shaw, of Stockton, who operated a foundry, and to Matteson & Williamson, Stockton implement dealers.

These new patent holders added more improvements, including wheels, reversible plow shares, and levelers to adjust the depth of plowing.

This version of the plow was manufactured and shipped to all parts of the world under the name of the Stockton Gang Plow.

It was years before a plow was built that allowed a teamster to ride instead of walking beside the plow.

Chapter 35

The Forming of the Ranchos

'It was the golden days of the dons'

The period of the 1830's was a confused and difficult one in California. Countless revolutions were taking place with radically extreme groups seeking power. Many men claimed to be governor, all at the same time, but none had the power with which to govern.

In 1831, Governor Echeandia announced his plan to secularize the missions and free the Indians. The missions would be taken out of the hands of the religious authorities, providing more land to give to rancheros. This ushered in the "Golden Days of the Dons".

During Spanish rule, only 20 ranchos were granted, half of them within 100 miles of Los Angeles. On the ranchos, cattle roamed freely without fences. Some say the entire state might still be owned by the descendants of roughly a dozen Spanish families had California not won independence from Mexico in 1846.

Those prophets came near to being correct, for even with independence, much of California's lands fell into the hands of only two American owners, one a cattle baron, and the other a railroad.

Under Mexican rule, any loyal citizen could ask for land. There were Englishmen, Scotsmen, and Americans asking for land grants. There were two main requirements. The applicant had to either marry a Mexican citizen or become one, and the applicant must belong to or join the Catholic Church.

Under Mexican law, any loyal citizen could ask the Governor for land. The request could be for as much as 50,000 acres, but not less than 4,500 acres. The applicant had to stipulate how much land he needed for his family and for cattle.

Land grants often went to soldiers who came to California with the occupation forces. As they retired from service, many turned to raising cattle on land grants given them for their loyal service on poor food and scant pay. With the grants of land, once poor soldiers overnight became Dons who lived like barons.

It was a great day when a new land grant was formally transmitted to a Ranchero. A formal survey would be made. It became a neighborhood affair. Anyone who wanted to view the landmarks could do so. Then, the Ranchero would pull up grass and small stones, throwing them to the four winds, signaling the "land was now his".

The Indians, who were freed by Mexico, were supposed to get a portion of the mission lands. Generally, they were cheated out of their shares. Those who did receive land, sold it for little or nothing, or found managing the property far beyond their abilities.

Father Antonio Horro said the Indians were no worse off after secularization of the missions than they were before. "Mission treatment shown to the Indians was the most cruel I have ever read in history," he said.

Great feudal estates were scattered along the coast south from what is Marin County today. Questions arising over titles to the Mexican land grants were to be one of the many factors leading to the demise of the great ranchos.

New arrivals to California challenged the land ownership and began squatting on unfenced lands of the ranchos. California's new immigrants refused to believe any single person could own so much land as existed under some of the Spanish land grants

The Treaty of Guadalupe Hidalgo committed the United States to giving full faith and credit to all of the acts under Mexico. This commitment meant that grants of land under Mexican rule were legal and authentic.

However, this stipulation covered only property that could be proved to have been acquired in California prior to July 7, 1846.

It wasn't unusual for a land parcel's description to read. "as bounded by the old dirt road," extending to "the prickly pear patch," and running from there to the "steer's skull" or "the tumbleweed," or "the small stone."

Most such descriptions ended with the phrase "mas o menos" or "more or less". Tumbleweeds move, sand may have buried both the steer's skull and the small stone, and settling land claims became difficult at best.

Some ranchos disintegrated because of The Great Drought of the 1860s. Little if any rain fell in 1860, and the years following were even worse, especially

1863 and 1864. Streams became small trickles, eventually turning to beds of dust.

Irrigation systems were useless because the source of water was gone. Cattle, the thing that had made the rancheros rich, began to die.

On the heels of the drought, money lenders surged into California, offering cash and taking mortgages in return. In a few years, land that had once belonged to the Spanish rancheros was passed through foreclosures to the bankers of San Francisco.

One firm, Pioche & Bayerque, charged an interest rate of five percent per month, compounded monthly. This soon became the going rate. Desperate rancheros were so eager to get money, lenders who had only a few hundred dollars to lend initially, ended up foreclosing on a large tract of land, themselves becoming wealthy.

Just before Mexican rule ended in California on July 7, 1846, Governor Pio Pico began handing out enormous grants of land in return for bribes.

Pio Pico could read the handwriting on the wall and wanted to amass as much wealth as possible for his imminent retirement from public life. Some Mexican officials, as well as private citizens, were said to conduct a lively business selling land grants over Governor Pico's forged signature.

In 1851, Congress passed an act to settle the private land claims in the State of California. All who claimed land were to appear before a land commission meeting in San Francisco. Many who owned land had lost proof of title or had boundaries so ill-defined that it was impossible to ascertain with any degree of certainty just where their lands lay.

This all added to the U.S. land commission's dilemma of verifying the grants that were legal and those that were not. In all, the land commission heard 813 claims in its four years of meetings, confirmed 521, rejected 273, and discontinued 19.

Henry Miller, a San Francisco butcher, was one of those who began acquiring land during the Big Drought of the 1860s. It isn't clear how he acquired much of his lands, but it is known that some of his most valuable business associates became employees of the Land Commission's office, the California government's executive departments, and both houses of Congress in Washington.

Miller, in partnership with Charles Lux, with whom he formed the giant Miller and Lux cattle empire, eventually owned 14,539,000 acres of prime land in California and southern Oregon. Miller liked to boast that he could ride from Mexico to the Oregon border without leaving his own land.

Californians, at the time, were often heard to say, "What land Miller doesn't own in California, the Southern Pacific Railroad does." Indeed, the two did own nearly one-third of the land in the state, Miller with 14,500,000 acres and the Southern Pacific with 16,387,000 acres. The entire state had 101,563,523 acres.

Immigration to California slowed because of the land situation. There was little land to acquire for farming or other purposes. The railroad offered land for sale, but at exorbitant prices.

The small farmer without enough money to purchase a 100-acre farm, could easily acquire a mortgage from the railroad company. When a farmer couldn't make his mortgage payment, the railroad company just as happily foreclosed.

The railroad's large land holdings very nearly amounted to its undoing.

The Southern Pacific needed an expanding population to produce goods, livestock, and products that would be shipped by rail. The railroad company had anticipated that cities would spring up from California wilderness, but with so much land in the railroad's hands, there was no place for cities to be built.

The allure of California proved stronger than the lack of land, causing a surge in tenant farming. The huge tracts of land owned by Miller and by the Southern Pacific were in large part hard to manage.

The owners readily rented the land to tenant farmers, preferring to collect rents rather than till the land themselves. Tenant farming is still a mainstay in California's economy today.

Chapter 36

The Need for News

'Newspapers opened and quickly went broke'

California's two pioneer weeklies, the Californian, and the California Star, ceased publication once the gold rush started.

This influx of people rushing to California in search of gold also stimulated a newfound interest in news, prompting the publishers of the two closed-down papers to merge and reopen.

On January 4, 1849, the two newspapermen issued the celebrated successor of the two earlier papers, the Alta California. For more than 20 years, this newspaper enjoyed a preeminent place in California journalism, before going into decline in the 1870's and finally passing out of existence in the 1880's.

Two other San Francisco newspapers came on the scene in 1849. The Pacific lasted only two years, while Prices Current, died within 12 months.

The publishing battle continued. By 1854, San Francisco had 22 newspapers and journals. In 1850, a competitor to Alta California came on the scene in the form of John Nugent, who started the Daily Herald.

The Herald was nearly ruined by its forthright stand against the vigilantes, but it gradually recovered its advertisers, and lasted until 1862.

Despite the high mortality rate, additional newspapers crowded into the field. The capital needed to start a newspaper was not great, but San Francisco had become a fierce competitive jungle for readers and advertisers, making a newspaper's survival tenuous at best.

In the early 1850's, San Francisco's 12 dailies boasted a combined circulation of 15,000, exceeding those of London. Newspaper publishing wasn't limited to San Francisco, however.

During the 10-year period following the discovery of gold, Marysville and Jackson each had seven newspapers; Columbia, five; and San Andreas, Sonora and Mariposa, three each. By 1854, fifty-seven newspapers and periodicals within California served an average of 290,000 readers.

It was the Overland Monthly that received the most national acclaim. Bret Harte was its editor for a period, and attracted nationwide attention with his short stories, including "M'liss", "The Luck of Roaring Camp", and "The Outcasts of Poker Flat".

A host of other writers gained local recognition. These included Lieutenant George Derby, who wrote under the pen names of Squibob and John Phoenix. Derby was characterized as a practical joker.

When Derby became engaged, he told both his fiancee and his mother, each privately, that the other was totally deaf. Derby then left them together to shout at each other until they caught onto his prank.

Southern California, too, had its newspapers, the main ones being the San Diego Herald, which soon

179

became the Union, and the Los Angeles Star, the predecessor of the Times.

As readers may already know, the writer who gained the greatest and most lasting fame in the period was Samuel Clemens, under his celebrated pseudonym, "Mark Twain".

As a reporter in San Francisco, Clemens wrote openly about graft among the city's politicians. He named names. The San Francisco police became so unhappy with him, Twain was virtually forced to take refuge in the hills near Angel's Camp.

It was in Angel's Camp that Twain wrote his famous "The Jumping Frog of Calaveras County". He later visited Hawaii, traveled to Europe, and when he returned, found himself in great demand as a storyteller and writer, based mainly on his story of the Calaveras Jumping Frog contest.

Twain was able to make the transition that Bret Harte couldn't and left California to become a literary legend in his lifetime and beyond.

Before the completion of the transcontinental telegraph in 1861, the news found in these publications was weeks, and even months, old.

The importance of newspapers to the populace is supported by the growth of individual papers. Weeklies increasingly became dailies, and were generally published six times a week. There was no edition published on Monday.

Michael and Charles DeYoung established the San Francisco Chronicle in 1865 as a theatrical journal. During the next year, the Chronicle dropped the word "Dramatic" from its masthead and, by printing "telegraphic news" was soon on its way to becoming an important general paper.

Journalism continued to flourish elsewhere as the population grew. The Sacramento Bee was founded in 1857 by the father of Charles K. McClatchy. But it was the young McClatchy that gave new life to the Sacramento Bee.

The political philosophies of the Hearsts, with the San Francisco Examiner, the McClatchys, Thomas Storke, who opened the Santa Barbara News Press, and General Harrison Gray Otis, who acquired the L.A. Times in 1881, were often quite different.

They all, however, built substantial and influential newspapers that were vigorously involved in the issues of their times.

Chapter 37

Black Gold

Ten million barrels gushed from one well before it controlled'

Edward Doheny seemed like anything but an oil man. He had worked as a booking agent, a fruit packer, a mule driver, and as a singing waiter.

Other writers were even less generous. One listed him as a miner and a roustabout, while another noted that Doheny had acted as a procurer of young ladies for the traveling drummers who stopped at the Occidental Hotel in Wichita, Kansas.

He seldom stayed in one area long, and his wanderings include stops in Texas, Arizona, New Mexico, and Mexico, sometimes hitting small gold strikes, but generally ending up broke. Rumor had it that he once killed a man, and possibly more.

He was 36-years old when he arrived in Los Angeles in 1892, near penniless. In one of his never-ending strokes of luck, Doheny noticed a black man with a wagonload of black, steaming, tarry liquid.

On inquiry, he was told the tarry material was "brea", which bubbled from a pit on the edge of town. The poor families of Los Angeles scooped the tar from the pit, at no charge, for use as fuel.

Doheny instinctively knew the "brea" was crude oil. He went looking for and found the bubbling pit. The site is variously listed by historians as Hancock Park and Westlake Park.

Doheny was able to borrow money to lease the land, but had no money left to buy or lease a drill. With pick and shovel, he sunk a four-by-six-foot shaft into the ground.

A prospector friend soon joined him in the venture. Together, the two were eventually able to employ a well driller.

At 600 feet, oil gushed forth, making it the first real gusher found in California. This brought a rush of oil prospectors to the area. Anyone who could get together the $1,500 cost of digging a well began leasing land west of downtown Los Angeles.

It was like Titusville, Pennsylvania, when oil was first discovered there.

More than 3,000 wells in the Los Angeles basin were pumping oil by 1899, all from a narrow tract of land varying from 800 to 1500 feet wide and four-and-a-half-miles long.

The frenzy of drilling caused Los Angeles city fathers to declare that oil wells were a civic nuisance. A moratorium was pronounced on further drilling within city limits.

This did not cause drilling to cease, however. Now, virtually everyone in the city seemed to need a new water well. The city council could hardly deny a citizen the right to have water. If the water well just happened to spout oil, who could have predicted it. It was simply a freak of nature.

Soon, oil shipped out of Los Angeles glutted the market. The cost of drilling exceeded the price each barrel returned. The oil boom was followed by panic and oil leases went begging for buyers.

Again, Ed Doheny seemed to be in the right place when the oil business succumbed to panic.

He quietly began buying up leases at bargain-basement prices. "Why," he asked, "did the oil market have to be limited to Southern California?"

His reasoning seemed sound. Los Angeles, after all, had a major port, which Titusville, Pennsylvania, did not. Doheny had visions of controlling California's entire oil production within 10 years.

Doheny was able to persuade the Santa Fe Railroad to switch from coal to oil to power its great engines, which boosted his fortunes considerably.

"Dry Hole Charlie" Woods hit a gusher north of Maricopa on March 15, 1910. His nickname instantly changed to "Gusher Charlie". The blast from this well was so tremendous that the derrick disappeared into the crater.

It took weeks to bring the gusher under control. To control the oil, an earthen dam was built around it, high enough to smother the gusher in a lake of its own oil.

For the next 18 months, the flow of Charlie's well was estimated at 15,000 to 68,000 barrels a day, eventually amounting to some ten million barrels from a single well.

In 1920, Shell Oil Company took a lease on Signal Hill and began to drill. The company decided to stop drilling operations at Alamitos Number One. It sent a telegram to its crews there to stop drilling. The crews failed to get the message.

The following day, Signal Hill became one of the richest oil producing areas in the state.

Chapter 38

A Billy the Kid Tale

'Rumors were rampant, and this one ran wild'

While William "Billy the Kid" Bonney was never in California, the rumor persisted that he once was. Billy, who had killed twenty one men by the time he reached the age of twenty one, became something of a Robin Hood character in Western folklore.

A number of groundless rumors surrounded the happenings of Billy the Kid. There were tales he "had escaped to Mexico", then "lived in disguise in the Pecos Valley", and also that he had "fled to Arizona".

The California yarn was that the ghost of Billy lived in the Panamint Valley in a half-deserted mining town. The rumor apparently started because living in this desert town was an old man referred to only as "The Kid".

The white bearded man was in his eighties, stood about five feet, eight inches tall, and had very small hands, which had turned shaky with age. Despite his age and stature, The Kid could whip out a six-shooter and put six bullets in a target with astounding accuracy.

The man was very secretive about his past, and never discussed Billy the Kid, nor never ever claimed to be him. Neither did he deny it. He would only insist that he had been "The Kid" for eighty years and "The Kid" he intends to remain.

When asked what he did in New Mexico, he merely answered he had punched some cattle, worked for some of the big cattlemen, and somehow, always managed to add, "And I learned how to handle a gun."

One man who knew about Bob Ollinger, a so-called bad man in the 1880s, was chatting with The Kid one day. Ollinger was said to have been jealous of Billy the Kid. While Billy was in jail in New Mexico, Ollinger would taunt him about how it would feel when young Billy was hanged the next day.

Billy didn't hang. Instead, he got hold of a deputy's gun, killed him, and escaped.

When the old man they called "The Kid" in Panamint Valley was asked about Ollinger, he pulled out his revolver, aimed at a tin can, and emptied his gun, saying, "He's right there where that tin can is settin'!":

The Kid fired the revolver six times, causing the can to jump each time. To that, he added, "Hello, Bob. An take that to hell with you?"

As both men became quiet, The Kid scratched the back of his neck, and calmly asked, "Ollinger, did you say? Nope. Don't recollect that I ever heard of him."

Chapter 39

Will Rogers, The People's Choice

He could make people laugh by making fun of them

The following columns were taken from the writings of Will Rogers, composed while he was in California.

Bishop, August 30, 1932:
"California always did have one custom that they took serious, but it amused the rest of the United States. That was in calling everything a "ranch". Everything big enough to spread a double mattress on is called a "ranch".

Well, up here is these mountains where there is lots of fishing, why every house you pass they sell fishing worms, and it's called a "worm ranch".

"Well, I always did want to own a "ranch", so I am in the market for a good worm ranch. I never was so hot as a cowboy, but I believe I would make a good "worm herder".

If I can land our Presidents as clients, I could make it sound like England when they sell to the king, "Rogers worm ranch, purveyor to His Excellency, the President.

187

Beverly Hills, September 6:

"Don't miss seeing the building of Boulder Dam. It's the biggest thing that's ever been done with water since Noah made the flood look foolish. You know how big the Grand Canyon is. Well, they just stop up one end of it, and make the water come out through a drinking fountain.

"They are only bothered with two things: One is silt and the other is senatorial investigations. They both clog everything up. It's called "Hoover Dam" now, subject to election returns of November 8.

"The dam is entirely between Nevada and Arizona. All California gets out of it is the water."

Beverly Hills, September 9:

"Eighty-two years ago today California entered the Union, on a bet. The bet was that the country would eventually be called California and not America.

"We took it away from Mexico the next year after we found it had gold. When the gold was all gone we tried to give it back, but Mexico was too foxy for us. In '49 the wayward sons out of 10,000 families crossed the country, and the roads were so rough they couldn't get back."

Chapter 40

Sutter Builds a Fort

'Everything He Did Went Wrong'

Johann August Sutter was a German-Swiss merchant, who left Europe, abandoning his family to escape debtor's prison.

Like his European experiences, Sutter failed just as badly at his American business ventures. He was said to be something of a linguist, and became fluent in Spanish while traveling the southwest.

Sutter found his way to Hawaii by way of a Hudson's Bay Company ship. While there, he convinced an American merchant to let him have a ship for a trading expedition to California.

He traveled to California by way of Sitka, Alaska, taking the trouble to gather letters from British, American, and Russian officials along the way.

Sutter used the letters he had collected to convince Governor Juan Bautista Alvarado that he would be a valuable man to have in California.

He asked Governor Alvarado for land so he could settle in the Sacramento Valley. His rancho would become a buffer zone against the Indians as well as against the Americans coming over the mountains. Alvarado granted him eleven square leagues of land.

Sutter had brought with him from Hawaii eight "kanaka" laborers, and two of their wives, as well as three Anglos. He established a fort where the city of Sacramento is today.

From these headquarters, Sutter took possession of a 50,000-acre tract of land in the Sacramento River Valley. He became a Mexican citizen and fully intended to carve out a princely empire.

Wearing a general's uniform, which he favored, Sutter called his establishment New Helvetia (New Switzerland) and maintained an army at the fort.

John Sutter put everyone to work, Hawaiians, Americans, Indians, Californios, as he developed his empire. He acquired an additional two leagues of land from later Governor Manuel Micheltorena, and claimed a lot more simply because no one else had.

He acquired cattle, and dealt in beaver skins, lumber, and agricultural products. Sutter's Fort was on the direct east-west route and became a convenient stopping place for travelers.

Sutter sent relief expeditions to rescue the Donner Party that was stranded and starving in a meadow beside the Truckee River. He hoped his aid would allow them to finish their trek over the Sierras.

Sutter eventually lost everything he had to the gold seekers swarming into California and across his land. Several thousand squatters moved in on the unfortunate Swiss' 11-square-league land grant. Those people who had purchased land from him held title legally, but others settled on land they had not bought.

In August 1850, some of the squatters' leaders were arrested. This only caused the squatters to band together in an army to free their leaders. In the melee that followed, the mayor and sheriff of Sacramento were shot and killed, and it was evident that law and order would not prevail in Sacramento.

In his old age, Sutter, living in Pennsylvania, petitioned the United States Congress for a pension, but the Supreme Court disallowed his claim.

Chapter 41

The Wheatland Farmworker Riot

'More than 3800 workers appeared to fill 1500 Jobs'

The Wheatland riot of August 3, 1913, occurred at the Durst ranch, north of Sacramento, near the town of Wheatland.

Durst reportedly advertized for 2800 farm workers when his ranch needed only 1500. More than 3800 destitute workers of all races descended on the farm. There were Hindus, European imigrants and native Americans jostling for places in the work force.

Among those thousands appearing at the Durst ranch were union organizers for the Industrial Workers of the World (IWW), which had made previous attempts to organize farm workers.

The I.W.W.'s concentration was on organizing the white worker population, not because of racism, but because the next largest group, the Japanese, were said to be clannish and had formed their own associations for dealing with employers.

Chief among the union's organizers was IWW leader Richard "Blackie" Ford, who had formed an

192

IWW local of about 30 farm workers. Ford demanded that Durst negotiate wages and working conditions.

He then used his oratorical skills at a meeting in the workers' area on the night of August 3, where he urged them to rebel against the poor living conditions, lack of toilet facilities, and absence of drinking water in the fields among other things.

As the meeting was closing with spirited songs, the sheriff of Yuba County, the district attorney, and a posse arrived to break up the meeting and arrest Ford.

As the arresting procedure was taking place, a shot rang out, reportedly from the gun of a sheriff's deputy who hoped to quiet the crowd. The shot ignited a riot in which the sheriff, the district attorney, and at least two workers were killed.

In the following days, the area was patrolled by the state militia. The William J. Burns detective agency was hired to bring in the "Wobblies," as the IWW was called, from all over the state.

Blackie Ford was located and rearrested. Herman Suhr, another organizer, was found in Arizona, and without extradition proceedings, unceremoniously returned to California.

Both Ford and Suhr were tried for their roles in the so-called Wheatland riot, found guilty of murder, and given life sentences. Other IWW members were given shorter sentences.

Subsequent to the riot, a commission was established to look into health and sanitation facilities in labor camp housing. The commission was charged with the duty of inspecting labor camps to see that minimum standards of health and sanitation were observed.

The Wheatland incident did not produce any lasting improvements in working or living conditions for migratory laborers and their families, but it did result in the first law concerning the welfare of itinerant workers.

The IWW, however, had little appeal among the farm workers, and the union was never able to organize workers in agriculture.

About the Author

Alton Pryor has been a writer for magazines, newspapers, and wire services, as well as a free lance writer for more than 35 years.

He worked for United Press International as a reporter, both for the printed press and for radio media.

He was editor for a special weekend home and ranch section for the Salinas Californian for five years.

In 1963, he moved to California Farmer Magazine to the post of field editor, specializing in agricultural news and feature writing for the next 27 years.

Since leaving California Farmer, he has been a freelance writer, with published features in Golf Course Management Magazine, the national publication of golf course superintendents, as well as in Western Horseman Magazine and various California and Oregon agricultural journals.

He is owner and president of Stagecoach Publishing in Roseville, California.

199

Order Form

Fax orders: (916) 791-6340

Postal orders: Stagecoach Publishing, Alton Pryor, 5360 Campcreek Loop, Roseville, Ca. 95747-8009 (916) 771-8166

Please send _____ copies of Little Known Tales in California History.

Name:_____

Address:_____

City: _____State:_____Zip:_____

Telephone: (____)_____

Price $9.95
Shipping and handling: $3.00 for first book, and $1.00 each additional book.

Please enclose check or money order.